A LONG WAY TO TIERRA DEL FUEGO

A LONG WAY TO TIERRA DEL FUEGO

TERESITA DURKAN

VERITAS

First published 1999 by
Veritas Publications
7/8 Lower Abbey Street
Dublin 1

Copyright © Teresita Durkan 1999

ISBN 1 85390 510 0

British Library Cataloguing
in Publication Data.
A catalogue record for
this book is available
from the British Library.

Cover photograph used by kind permission of Alo Connaughton
Cover design by Bill Bolger
Printed in the Republic of Ireland by Betaprint Ltd, Dublin

*To the ancestors who launched me on this journey,
the family and friends who helped me on the way,
and Rebecca Perez Roldan
with whom I reached the shores of Tierra del Fuego in 1990,
this book is gratefully dedicated.*

You get the life you have the imagination for.
But where do you get the imagination?

CONTENTS

1

THE FROZEN PIRATE

It's a long way to Tierra del Fuego, especially if you start from the west of Ireland. Even if you set out from Valparaíso in central Chile, as I did in 1990, you still have almost three thousand kilometres to cover and some wildly beautiful places to see along the way. But if you set out, as I also did, from the village of Bunowen on the Atlantic coast of Mayo around the time of Hitler's war, the journey is bound to offer a great many more possibilities.

A small girl, determined, in her own imagination anyway, to follow the path of the sun across the ocean until she reaches the shores of Tierra del Fuego, has a long way to go. The scope for delays, detours, distractions, wanderings and even fully-fledged forgettings is nearly endless. Only the odd tenacity of the initial impulse and the circuitous ways of providence seem to keep the venture going. A great deal has to do with how the idea of the journey took shape in the first place, the mystery of origins and beginnings.

For me, at the start, it seemed a childishly simple project. It began, I suppose, when I was born in 1937 on a small farm near Louisburgh on the southern shores of Clew Bay, but I have no memory reaching back that far, so 1945 is a clearer starting point for me: 8 May, 1945.

It was a sunny day and had turned into a bright warm evening. There were tiny white blossoms on the hawthorn and big yellow flowers on the flag-irises in the rushy field we called Nancy Heshtion's when I went down to round up the cows for milking just after the Angelus bell rang at six o'clock. None of us knew anymore who Nancy Heshtion was. Maybe she was an old lady who had died in the Famine. Her humpy field, long since one of ours, was low-lying and liable to flood up with river-water when there was a high tide. My father suffered many a backache trying to drain it. He said it was only fit for summer grazing, but you could see where ridges of potatoes had once been sown in some parts of it. I liked squelching through it in my bare feet in summertime because it was boggy and soft underfoot.

Smells of farm animals and the scent of decaying seaweed, washed up on the shore during a recent storm, lay heavy on the air as I drove the cows into the shed. When they were tied up and ready for milking, I combed my hair, put on my shoes and headscarf, and ran as fast as I could to get to the chapel in time for the rosary. My brother Liam was on the altar that week, in charge of the thurible for benediction. I'd have liked to have been an altar-server myself, to get a swing at that puffing thurible on the end of its long silvery chain, but, being a girl, I had to content myself with celebrating 'pretend' Masses by myself at home in the front room.

After the rosary a few of us were hanging around near the old weighbridge outside the courthouse when my brother Anthony, who was three years older than me and generally into mischief of some kind, broke away from the group and ran down the road to the Protestant church. He shinned up the high boundary wall like a cat and planted himself on top of one of the pillars. Then he spread his arms wide and made a zooming noise as if he were Rockfist Rogan on a bombing mission over Berlin. He waited until we got near the gate and then shouted down at us, 'The war is over, the war is over, the war is over'.

Sean Dunne told him to dry up; everybody knew the war was over. We hadn't heard much else all day, at home, in school, or around the town. Even at the rosary Father Morley had said prayers of thanksgiving because the war was over. It was VE Day: Victory in Europe. Hitler was dead. The Germans had surrendered, and everybody seemed to be relieved that the fighting had come to an end. Anthony jumped down off the wall and dared Sean Dunne to race him to the bridge and back. When they were gone Joe Scanlan said to me, 'Anyway the war isn't over at all yet. The Americans are still fighting the Japs out there in the Pacific. They'll win too. The Yanks are *big*.'

He made it sound as if the Americans were giants and the Japanese were leprechauns. I wanted the Americans to win. I had seven aunts, my father's sisters, in America, and more cousins than I could count. Some of the aunts sent us parcels of clothes and cheques to my father at Christmas time. America, for us, was the land of plenty. Ireland was still a place where nearly everything was scarce except the rain.

'What difference will it make that the war is over?' I asked my mother when I got back to the house. She was just in from milking so I helped her to strain the warm new milk into shining black earthenware crocks. Then we scalded and filled the milk-jugs. Later on she'd have to skim the milk and gather the cream into one bigger vessel to get it ready for Friday's churning.

'Oh, it'll make many a difference.' she said. 'There'll be no more bombs falling on defenceless cities, and no more homeless and starving people wandering the roads of Europe. There'll be no more rationing or scarcities either, please God. The soldiers and prisoners-of-war will be able to go back to their own homes… and Alice and Annie Margaret will come home for holidays this summer too.'

That was the real news. Alice and Anne were my two oldest sisters. They had gone to England when I was small because there were no jobs for them after they finished school. My mother cried bitterly the day Anne left Bunowen in 1943. She had been trying to put off the moment when the first of our family would have to leave Ireland for good.

'It's not right to let any little girl into a country that's in the middle of a war,' she said accusingly to my father. 'There are bombs falling every night of the week on those cities in England.' It sounded as if she were blaming him for it. And he, who didn't want Anne to leave Bunowen either – she was probably the only one of us who went out willingly to help him on the land – said angrily to my mother, 'Tell me woman, how are you going to make her stop here?'

In the end nobody stopped her. She went first to Skipton, a little town in the Dales of Yorkshire where my mother's younger sister Aunt Bridgie ran a small hotel. That destination eased my parents' minds a little bit. It didn't seem like a place where too many bombs might fall. Alice followed her to Skipton a few months later, and not long after that they both moved down to the south of England where Anne trained as a nurse and Alice got work as a teacher.

The news that my two sisters would be coming home for holidays in summer was the best thing I had heard for ages. I felt like giving a hop, step and jump across the kitchen floor, out the front door, and down to the sea. I liked to go down there when I had something special to think about. But it was supper time so I had to stay in the house.

I had good reason to be excited, though. Now the nine of us – or twelve if you counted my father and mother and Aunt Maggie who was the only one of my father's sisters who didn't go to America because she had a lame step, and kept a little sweet-shop on the Square – would all be together again. Even Christmas hadn't been the same for me since Alice and Anne had gone away, so I was happy now just thinking about them coming home in the summer. When my mother asked me to go out and feed the calves I didn't complain, although it was Anthony's turn, and feeding the calves was a slow, mouthy, messy, drooly business that we all avoided if we could.

My father, who had been moulding potatoes in a field near the house, was finishing his supper when I came in with the empty buckets. He took up *The Irish Press* and pushed his chair into the little circle of light under the oil-lamp hanging from the centre of the kitchen ceiling. When he began to read the newspaper it was understood that we all had to stop making noise. So when the supper-table was cleared I sat down quietly and did my homework. It didn't take long. I was in a hurry to get it finished because I had a good book to read.

Uncle Rudolf, who was married to my mother's sister, Sarah, often sent us gifts of books from Bradford. This small, foreign-looking uncle – at least that's how I thought of him because in a photograph he looked tiny and swarthy beside our tall fair aunt – was a native of Burgdorf in Switzerland. He could speak several languages which was a wonder to us youngsters, though we secretly felt we had one small edge on him because he didn't know any Irish and we were learning it in school. The books he sent were thoroughly appreciated. We were keen readers and there was no public library in Louisburgh yet. He had just sent us this new sea-story called, I think, *The Frozen Pirate*.

It was a strange story, about a pirate ship – or maybe it was a captured Spanish galleon, I had a real fancy for Spanish galleons – that was driven off course in the stormy waters of the South Pacific. The ship was battered by icy winds and then lost its way in a freezing fog as it tried to make its way around the tiny island of Cape Horn at the tip of Tierra del Fuego. It finished up stuck fast in the ice somewhere along the edge of the big white continent of Antarctica.

But the captain and his crew didn't die. They were just frozen solid inside the ship and preserved alive, strange motionless ice-shrouded figures like statues, stuck fast to the spot where each of them had been standing or sitting or lying. Years later, or maybe it was decades or centuries later, the ice melted, the ship drifted into warmer waters and the captain and his crew woke up. They just thawed out and began to breathe and move around again without realising how long they had been asleep. But when they set about sailing their battered ship back to the Caribbean island that was their pirate-base, they found themselves, like Rip Van Winkle, in an unfamiliar world. Nobody recognised them. Nobody had ever heard of them. Nobody even knew that they had once been dangerous pirates on the Spanish Main.

It was a far-fetched tale, even for a credulous eight-year-old. But there was something vivid and realistic about the story's setting. Images of a frozen blue-and-white world surrounded by dangerous seas and storm-lashed islands like Cape Horn and Tierra de Fuego were planted in my mind for the first time. These images took hold in my imagination and would never fully leave it.

Not long after that I heard about a man from our village who went to Patagonia when my father was young. Nobody knew much about him except that he had left Bunowen a great many years ago and lived most of his life in South America. Shortly after the Second World War, news came to his family in Louisburgh that he had died suddenly in Buenos Aires and left a legacy to his Irish relatives. Someone said that he had worked for a while on the island of Tierra del Fuego.

I think that was when I asked my sister Sarah to show me those three places on the map; Buenos Aires, Tierra del Fuego and Patagonia. We had no trouble finding Buenos Aires. The capital of Argentina stood out clearly, a large red dot on the edge of the map. Tierra del Fuego was easy to find too, the big island that was like a crooked pointy toe at the foot of South America, but we couldn't see Patagonia anywhere in Sarah's small atlas.

I remember thinking that day while we were looking at Tierra del Fuego on the map, that it would probably be only a short trip from there to the shores of the big white continent of Antarctica. You could make a fairly straight run from one of those coasts to the other, I thought, like going from Louisburgh to Clare Island or Innishturk. After all, the frozen pirate and his crew had been blown from Cape Horn to Antarctica during a storm. It would be years – in fact the best part of five decades – before I finally got that very misleading idea about the distance between Tierra del Fuego and the shores of Antarctica out of my head.

It wasn't surprising, in retrospect, that my sister and I couldn't find Patagonia in a small Irish school atlas back in the 1940s. A great many years later when I sat down to plan the journey that would bring me, at last, to the shores of Tierra del Fuego, I still had trouble figuring out exactly where and what Patagonia was.

On the face of it there shouldn't be a problem. Patagonia, after all, is the largest and best-known geographical region in the south of Argentina, a vast territory that covers five administrative provinces. It's also well-known as the windiest, most desolate and most sparsely-populated region in that big country, besides being one of the most legendary and bleakly-picturesque landscapes in the whole of South America. So the place we were looking for had mythical as well as historical and geographical dimensions. Patagonia was a region on the map, but it was also what poets might call a country of the mind, a territory extending well beyond the boundaries of any particular province or political area, and that was probably why it was so hard to trace precisely on a map.

For one thing, it crosses a remote sweep of the Andes and gives its name to enormous stretches of southern Chile as well as to a large part of Argentina. Uniquely among South American territories, it has coasts on both the Atlantic and the Pacific. The long and desolate ridge of mountains that forms a much-disputed boundary between Chile and Argentina along these latitudes is called La Cordillera Patagonica. More than anything else, though, Patagonia is famous for having been, over many centuries, the scene of an almost unique human relationship with one of the planet's most challenging landscapes. Up to the beginning of the twentieth century it was the inhospitable homeland of several now-vanished indigenous tribes. Tapering off into the most southerly extreme of the Americas, this wild, islanded, headlanded, mountainous, barren, windy territory is the kind of place where even the great Andes have to bow to the inevitable and sink reluctantly into the sea.

Tierra del Fuego, at the most southerly tip, was the part of Patagonia that first attracted my attention to this faraway corner of the world. I thought, to start with, that it was just one big oddly-shaped island, but I gradually realised what an intricate and complex archipelago it really is. Its southernmost tip is the tiny storm-lashed island of Cape Horn, dreaded for centuries by the crews of sailing ships. A rocky, foggy island surrounded by waters awash with icebergs, it remains a permanent sailing hazard and, in certain weathers, a navigator's nightmare. Some nostalgic Dutch mariners gave it its name, not because it reminded them of a horn, but because Hoorn was the place they came from in the distant, unruffled flatlands of Holland.

Patagonia seems to have cast a powerful spell over the minds of European explorers and adventurers almost from the time it first appeared as a shadowy territory on maps of the New World. One of the oddest chapters in its history took place in the middle of the nineteenth century when a Frenchman called Orelie-Antoine de Tounens hailed it as a kingdom and claimed as his own. This obscure lawyer from the French provinces set out for South America to make himself a king. He left Paris in the 1860s to conquer the Araucanian regions of southern Chile, and eventually added the name of Patagonia to his shadowy dominions, probably to give his title a more resounding ring. The Chilean government saw to it that his efforts to carve a kingdom out of their hard-won national territory came to nothing. Even so, a successor to his royal titles is said to maintain a consular office in Paris to this day.

When Generals Bernardo O'Higgins and Jose San Martin led their armies of liberation across the Andes from Argentina, and freed Chile from Spanish rule at the beginning of the nineteenth century, Patagonia and Tierra del Fuego were divided between the two newly-independent states. The division remained sketchy in some places because the remoter areas in this part of South America hadn't yet been accurately mapped. This was to lead to boundary conflicts and unfriendly squabbles between the two countries that have lasted, on and off, for nearly two hundred years. Threats of war, troop-mobilisations, diplomatic and undiplomatic notes and declarations, armed stand-offs, and occasional agreements mediated by neutral third parties such as the Pope, have all been resorted to in order to settle Chile's and Argentina's competing claims to what, by any standards, must be some of the most barren, ice-bound and unfertile territories in the world. A vast frozen wilderness called the Fields of Ice is still one of the areas at the centre of an ongoing dispute. It seems that external relations between Chile and Argentina wouldn't be quite normal if at least one of these eternal territorial wrangles weren't in progress.

But I knew nothing about all this when I first became interested in Patagonia. Its political and territorial extension, the complexities of its history, the tragic story of its indigenous tribes, and the strange allure that this remote part of South America has had for Europeans over the centuries, were beyond my ken when I first started turning the word Patagonia around in my mind, in the 1940s, as a place I'd one day like to visit. On the other hand, I had images and fantasies of my own about the place. Indeed it's quite possible to have vivid dreams and pleasing desires about things of which one is wonderfully ignorant.

I had overheard a conversation on the Bunowen road once, when I was about ten years old, that gave me my first idea of what Patagonia might be like. We were on our way home from picking carrageen at the shore, and two neighbours started talking about people from Mayo who had emigrated to unusual parts of the world, meaning places different from England and America where west-of-Ireland people usually went. Kimberley in South Africa and Kalgoorlie in Australia were two of the places they mentioned.

'And a few fellows from here even got as far as Patagonia,' one of them said.

I pricked up my ears. We had just passed the house of the Bunowen man who died in Buenos Aires, leaving a legacy to his relatives. Some people said he had made his money in Patagonia or Tierra del Fuego.

'Aye. Back then there was a lot of talk about that part of the world. They went down there looking for gold.'

'Wasn't there supposed to be another Klondike or Eldorado in it, or something?'

'So they said. But sure it was only a wild rumour,' the first man said.

'I never heard of anyone that made a fortune at gold-mining down there. Did you?'

'Not from around here anyway.'

The other man laughed, 'But that didn't stop them going looking for it, I suppose.'

'Maybe they thought it was going to be another Yukon. With gold-nuggets in every stream. I remember when I was a young lad we had a rhyme we sang in the school yard:

> Goodbye to spuds and buttermilk.
> I'll soon be on me way
> To Terry del Few-ay-go
> In South Ame-ri-kay.

'But sure most of those poor fellows ended up working on the big sheep and cattle stations at the cold end of Argentina. That was how they earned their passage up to the States, or round again to Buenos Aires.'

'So Patagonia was no great shakes after all?'

'And Tierra del Fuego was a wild cold place too, by all accounts.'

One of the men noticed that I was listening. He smiled at me and said, 'So, there you are now. Tierra del Fuego is an awful long way from Bunowen.'

'How would you get there?' I asked him.

He frowned and looked puzzled for a minute. Then he said, 'You'd better ask the nun about that in school tomorrow. She'll be able to show it to you on the map. It's away down there at the tail end of South America. I'm telling you no lie. It's an awful long way from Louisburgh. There's fierce wide stretches of the Atlantic ocean between here and Tierra del Fuego.'

And that, in its own vague, expansive way, helped to keep me on the trail.

2

THE PATH OF THE SUN

As a child I loved not only the sea but every song, poem, rhyme or story that had anything to do with it. Ships, boats, voyages, distant oceans, shipwrecks, pirates, smugglers, remote islands, sunken treasures, old sagas and sea-adventures, tales of battles, storms, disasters and drownings – all these fed some inner impulse of curiosity, fantasy or imagination that was, in its own way, almost insatiable. Stories of shipwrecks, books like *Robinson Crusoe, The Swiss Family Robinson, Moby Dick* and *Treasure Island*, although they were my brothers' books, had no reader more avid in our house than me. And when films came to Louisburgh for the first time, in the 1940s, by far the most memorable pictures for me were *Captain Courageous, Mutiny on the Bounty* and *Black Beard, the Pirate*.

It didn't matter whether the stories I read were about ships that had really existed, like the great liners that still crossed the Atlantic with wealthy travellers and poor emigrants when I was a child, or the famous ships that had fought in the battles of naval history from Salamis and Trafalger to Jutland and the River Plate. I liked to play with words like brigs and frigates, galleons and caravels, flagships and ships-of-the-line, pirate sloops and schooners, clippers and windjammers, warships, cruisers, carriers and destroyers, and I tended to mix them all up with a relish that didn't distinguish very clearly between the different and sometimes menacing realities that lay behind them.

Phantom ships, legendary or ghostly vessels like *The Flying Dutchman*, the frozen pirate's ship, or the shadowy *Caleuche* had a special place in my imagination. I didn't care whether the vessels I read about were manned by smugglers or pirates, pig-tailed Chinamen, bronze-skinned Sandwich islanders, mysterious Parsees and Lascars, Nantucket whalers, or just ordinary 'baccy-chewing British tars. It was all the same to me, because every one of them was as vivid and alluring as, I suppose, Star Trekkers and space-voyagers are to youngsters of today.

I was one of the ones who sang loudest in school when Sister Cecilia taught us a song about an old Galway hooker called *The Queen of Connemara*:

> Oh, my boat can safely float in the teeth of wind and weather
> And outrace the swiftest hooker between Galway and Kinsale.
> When the dark floor of the ocean and the wild winds sweep about her.
> How she rides in her pride like a seagull in the gale!

It didn't matter that I had never seen such a boat myself, much less sailed in one. It was my curious and insistent fascination with the *idea* of boats and ships and going to sea that kept me interested.

So it was probably a throwback at a lonely and uncertain moment in my life that gave me the subject for one of the first jottings I made in my notebook after I arrived in Valparaíso in 1989. This was a run of doggerel-verse about the sea-going craft I could see – or fancied I could see – when I looked down from a viewing-point above the docks in Playa Ancha and tried to imagine what the black specks on the horizon might be, as they made their way into and out of the old harbour:

> Is it a destroyer or is it a cruiser?
> Is it a rowboat with a stiff rowlock?
> Is it a freighter with cranes and containers

or a flat-bottomed ferry with a maw like a box?
Is it a frigate, grey ship of the navy?
Is it a squat-tubbed submarine?
Is it a launch for tourist trippers
or a big fruit-transport, a floating fridge?
Is it a cruiseship from Hamburg or Bremen?
Is it the Queen Elizabeth Two?
Is it a US aircraft carrier,
here for manoeuvres and manned like a zoo?
Is it a yacht from the Viña marina,
a lighter, a tug, or a pilot boat?
Is it a trim little naval cutter
or a coalboat from Huasco with a cargo of coke?
Is it a tanker with oil from Caracas,
a lightship, a coaster, or just a decoy?
Is it a lifeboat, a Japanese whaler,
or a harbour patrol-boat checking the buoys...?

And so on until I ran out of categories. Although Valparaíso hadn't much left then of the thriving Pacific seaport that was prosperous and world-famous before the cutting of the Panama Canal, it was still a congenial place for someone who loved ships and the sea. And even now, in spite of its relative decay and poverty, it remains a happy hunting-ground for those who relish the salty atmosphere of old seaports, or care to wander among the lost worlds that are preserved under the glass-topped showcases of maritime and naval museums.

One of my favourite sea-writers, almost from the time I was old enough to read and understand him a little, was Joseph Conrad. *Nostromo*, his great novel about South America, is still one of my favourite books. I know no work of literature that re-creates so vividly the life of these old Pacific seaports, or evokes so powerfully the mercurial transitions of South American politics played out against the hypnotic landscapes of this great continent.

I had re-read *Nostromo*, for the third time I think, shortly before I left Ireland for Chile in 1989, and it seemed to me that I could meet the shadow of Joseph Conrad on many a street-corner in the decayed old port-sector of Valparaíso. I'd think of him especially as I walked along the docks and watched the much-scaled-down activities of the merchant shipping in the old harbour where, in his era, thousands of vessels had come and gone. Valparaíso was at the height of its fame and prosperity when Conrad sailed the Pacific as a master-mariner towards the end of the nineteenth century, and here he certainly made more than one welcome landfall.

But my fascination with ships and boats, when I was a child, had to nourish itself for a long time on a very slender diet of reality. I never saw a big ship, in real life, when I was small. And the only boats I was familiar with were the little tarred curraghs that were still used as fishing-craft along the west coast of Ireland during my childhood. Those light-ribbed wooden rowing-boats, waterproofed with tarred canvas, were good for a day's fishing, or for ferrying light loads to and from the islands, but they were too frail and open to the hazards of bad weather for almost anything else. Around Louisburgh we called them canoes.

In my grandparents' time nearly every family living near the sea had a canoe, or else they shared one with some of their neighbours. Fishing or harvesting something from the sea – winkles, dulse, carrageen, crabs, sand-eels, barnacles and the like – had often made the difference between starvation and survival for many of the big families who grew up along the west coast of Ireland during the hungry years that weren't by any means confined to times of historically-documented famine. So these light, tarry-black fishing boats were a very familiar part of my childhood. Dragged up for safety above the high water mark, and turned on their backs to let the rain run off them when they weren't in use, they looked for all the world like long black snails with down-turned snouts. These were all the sea-going craft I had ever known, at first hand, when I was a child.

Sometimes, in the distance, we might catch sight of a little fleet of fishing-trawlers crossing Clew Bay on their way to Murrisk or Westport, and as children we used to shout in great excitement, 'Look at the trawlers, the big boats.' In a way, I suppose, they were big by comparison with the tiny curraghs that fished out of our own local coves. Now and then during summer a light graceful vessel with a couple of white sails, which we thought of as a yacht, could be seen out sailing or anchored in the shelter of some local harbour when people like the Mountbattens or the Woodham-Smiths were holidaying in the area. But apart from that, I never saw anything that looked even remotely like the fine ships I was constantly coming across in my sea-stories and picture-books. In fact, it was one of the great disappointments of my childhood that the caravels and galleons, schooners and clippers, brigs and frigates that I read about in my sea-stories never seemed to put in an appearance anywhere near Clew Bay. The same was true of pirate ships and smuggling craft, as far as I could tell.

As for the great liners and luxury-cruisers that sailed from Bremen and Cherbourg, Southampton and Cobh to ports like New York and Saint John, I knew that they belonged to a different world. But it too was a world that held a strong fascination for me, so it was a special excitement whenever my mother took me with her on a visit to her old home in Pulgloss, a place where boats had actually been built, and passages were still booked for voyages on some of those great transatlantic liners.

My grandfather found me one day with my nose pressed hard against the glass-fronted bookcase in the sitting room of the old family house in Pulgloss. I was peering at the pictures of ships that were folded away among the books and magazines on one of the lower shelves. My longing to get at those books and pictures was almost as intense as my urge to lay hands on the chocolate bars in my Aunt Maggie's sweetshop on The Square in Louisburgh. But the sweetshop was a place I passed every day on my way to school, whereas Pulgloss was a village some miles southwest of Louisburgh across the Bunowen river, and I only got to spend time there whenever my mother picked me as the one to bring with her when she went on a visit to her old home.

My mother's father, Anthony MacHale, was an agent in a small way for the Cunard and White Star shipping lines. He booked passages for people who were emigrating to America. It was a steady little business except when emigration to the United States was interrupted by the two World Wars. I was a captive to the spell of those great ships, on which many of my relatives and neighbours sailed away to a foreign land, and there was nothing that brought me closer to them than the books and pictures in my grandfather's bookcase.

Among these pictures, there was one attractive fold-out of *The Titanic*. My grandfather spread it on the table one day in the sitting room and said, 'I suppose you know all about this famous ship and what happened to her?'

I nodded shyly, 'The biggest liner ever built. She was sunk by an iceberg in the north Atlantic on her maiden voyage to New York.'

'That's right,' he said, 'and it happened just thirty-two years ago, in April 1912. Now I'm going to tell you a little story you mightn't know. Did anyone ever tell you that your Uncle John came within an ace of being a passenger on board that great liner when she went down?'

I shook my head, and then listened with great interest as he told us the story.

'Well, it's true. John had been talking about going to America since the beginning of 1911, but I didn't want him to go so far away, and neither did his mother. He was barely twenty at the time. Intelligent, handsome, strong and well-built, six-foot-two in his stockings, and he had a fine head of dark wavy hair…'

I opened my eyes wide as I listened to my grandfather's description of that younger Uncle John. Whenever I thought about my uncle now I remembered very different things, like the half-crowns he gave me and my brothers and sisters when he came visiting to Bunowen, and the large amounts of whiskey and stout he and my father drank over their long talks in the sitting-room. I remembered his accent, which had an unfamiliar Belfast twang to it with odd words like 'yon' and 'thon' that we never used in Louisburgh. But most of all I remembered Uncle John for his big bald shiny pate. Sometimes I'd stand behind his chair just to get a better look at it. If there had been a competition for shiny bald heads, I'd certainly have given the first prize to Uncle John.

'You'd be better off applying to join the police and stop thinking about America,' his mother told him.

'Nobody had much grá for the police in Ireland at the time,' my grandfather explained. 'They were agents of English power in the country, and some of them weren't greatly liked or trusted, but it was a job with regular pay, and it was better to be a policeman in Ireland than a poor emigrant in America.'

So young John MacHale applied to join the Royal Irish Constabulary. He passed the entrance tests, but months went by and he wasn't called up for training, so he went back to his father and asked him to book a passage on *The Titanic*. He wanted to sail to the greatest city in the world, on the maiden-voyage of the biggest ship that had ever been built, since Noah's Ark anyway, he said. His parents were still against it but he insisted, and the booking was made.

'She was to sail at the beginning of April,' my grandfather told us, 'but God must have heard his mother's prayers. Early that same spring his call to the police came, and he was posted to a training depot in Dublin and then to Belfast. *The Titanic* sailed a while after that, and you all know what happened to her.'

I heard that story in 1944. Uncle John had left the police many years before, but he continued to live and work in Belfast and he eventually married and settled down there. He often spent summer holidays in the west of Ireland. His wife's family were the first Presbyterians I ever knew. I remember him as a jovial, generous uncle, a convivial, hard-drinking man, a raconteur who felt he had cheated the North Atlantic of his bones and meant to enjoy to the full the life he hadn't lost.

One of the many items of drinker's doggerel he was fond of quoting to my father or anyone else who'd listen to him when he was in his cups, said:

> Here lies a man who saved his all
> for the day that the rain and the snow might fall.
> He had no pleasures, he played no games –
> and he died before the blizzard came.

Uncle John wasn't going to let a fate like that overtake him if he could possibly help it. He survived *The Titanic* by about sixty years and died, an octogenarian, in his bed.

'There was another man called John MacHale who built boats here in Pulgloss a great many years ago,' my grandfather told us another day. He was sitting at the fire in the sitting room, talking to my mother, and I was at the table turning over the pages of a book that had pictures of old sailing ships in it. Those graceful old vessels seemed to me to be like great white seabirds that could speed across the surface of the ocean as if they had wings.

'Did he ever build a ship like any of these?' I asked him.

My grandfather threw back his head and laughed.

'Ships in Pulgloss, is it? Grand, tall, full-rigged vessels like those ones? Now, wouldn't that be a fine thing!' But he smiled and shook his head.

'No, there were never any big ocean-going vessels like that built around here. There wouldn't be a harbour anywhere along this coast deep enough to take them.'

'So what kind of ships did he build then?' I tried not to show how disappointed I felt.

'Oh, good sturdy boats for fishing, and strong vessels with sails for ferrying animals and heavy loads to and from the islands. The boat-building business in this family went back well over a hundred years.'

'Wasn't there a poem,' I asked, 'an Irish poem about a drowning disaster? A man from the west cursed this MacHale man who built a boat for his family, because she went down in a storm. Isn't that true?'

'Indeed it is,' my grandfather said, and he shook his head again, this time slowly and thoughtfully.

Afterwards I heard him saying to my mother in a low voice that I could barely hear, 'You know, some people believed that man's curse had something to do with... what happened to the young girl who went to America... afterwards,' and they exchanged glances that I couldn't understand.

'Go on down and have your tea now,' my mother said, and I recognised straightaway the tone she used whenever she wanted to get rid of me. I was the youngest and had a reputation for having sharp ears and lingering in quiet corners listening to things my elders thought I'd be better off not hearing. So they used to send me on messages, or tell me to go off and read my book or ride my bike, just when a conversation was beginning to get interesting. It never failed to annoy me and make me twice as curious as I was before and even more determined to get at the whole story anyway.

'Aunt May is making boxty, and there's hot scones and gooseberry jam too. So, off you go now, like a good girl, and play with your cousins, and have your tea,' and she whooshed me out of the sitting room without more ado. I had to leave the book of sailing ships behind me too. So I didn't hear what happened to the young girl who went to America, that evening, though I think I'd have been willing to do without the boxty and scones, and maybe even the gooseberry jam, just to hear the rest of the story.

It took me years to get that particular bit of family history out of my mother, and when she did tell me about it she was sad and vague, as if the events might have had a different ending that she didn't know, or didn't want to think of, or tell me about.

I finally heard the story when I was a teenager home from school for the long summer holidays in 1952. My aunts, Sarah and Bridgie, came visiting from Bradford and Skipton for a few weeks that summer. They were sitting in the kitchen in Bunowen with my mother drinking tea one evening when somebody brought up the subject of Innishturk. This little island off the Mayo coast, about nine miles southwest of Pulgloss, was a place where the MacHale family had cousins.

My mother and some of her sisters used to go visiting to Innishturk when they were young, and I knew that my mother had spent at least one memorable holiday on the island before she got married. I thought she must have had a secret romance there or met an island Romeo, because the place always seemed to call up a memory of happiness for her. Her features would take on a nostalgic glow and her talk about Innishturk always had a special warmth and affection in it. Besides, she had a great welcome for the island people whenever they came to the house if they were out in Louisburgh selling their sheep and cattle at the fair. My father, on the other hand, wasn't too enthusiastic about the island or the islanders, and he generally wasn't very pleased if any of them stayed over when they were marooned on the mainland by bad weather.

As for me, I thought that Innishturk must be the last place God made, a small humpy island far out in the sea. People said it was shaped like a *torc*, the Irish word meaning wild boar, from which it was supposed to have got its name. I thought of it as being miles away in the middle of the Atlantic, because to get at it you had to go first to one of the other islands – Clare Island or Innishboffin – and then wait until the mail boat or some other vessel was willing to take you the rest of the way. As a teenager, I was more into towns and cities than poor islands that smelled of the sea and fish and hardship.

'How did we come to have cousins living in Innishturk?' I asked the three tea-drinking ladies.

My real question was how would anyone want to live on a poor, out-of-the-way island like that if they had any other choice, even the unwelcome one of emigrating to England or America. Poverty was still a harsh reality in the west of Ireland when I was growing up, and even in the towns and cities to the east of us things weren't much better. But out on those little islands along the west coast there was often downright want and hardship. Most of those born on the islands when I was young got out of them as fast as they could, and went to England or America if they couldn't get work on the Irish mainland.

'Your grandfather's step-sister was married to a man from the island,' Aunt Sarah said.

It was Aunt Bridgie who asked the next question although something like it was on the tip of my own tongue.

'What in God's name was her father thinking of to let her marry into such a poor isolated spot? Surely to God he could have made a better match for her somewhere out here on the mainland?'

'Maybe it was because of what happened to his other daughter,' my mother said.

The events hadn't been much talked about when they were growing up, and they had very few solid details about what really happened. This is what they told me. A neighbour from another village came home from America on holidays some time around the turn of the century. This lady was full of stories about the good life people had in America, and the big money you could make there, and how easy everything was by comparison with the hardship and poverty in the west of Ireland. Maybe it was those stories that caught the attention of one of the young Pulgloss girls, or maybe she had already made up her mind that she wanted to emigrate anyway.

However it was, she persuaded her parents to let her go to America with this older neighbour when she was going back after her holidays. The lady promised to take good care of her until she arrived safely at the home of some family relatives who were living in Chicago. There was a farewell party in Pulgloss the night before she left, an American Wake they called it. The father saw his daughter off the next morning at the railway-station in Westport. It was a sad parting. She was the first member of the family to leave home, and she was going very far away. Emigrants to America in those days didn't often get to visit their homes and families again, unless they were lucky enough to make, or marry, a lot of money. Her father and mother took as much comfort as they could from the fact that their daughter was going to relatives, and that she wouldn't be making the long journey alone.

But that goodbye at Westport railway station turned out to be the last certain news they ever had of their daughter. It was also the point at which the story became an unsolved mystery. According to what her older companion reported afterwards, all went well until the ship docked in New York. When they disembarked and were going through the immigration queues on Ellis Island, the young girl was put into a different section from the older woman because she was a first-time immigrant and the older lady was returning from a visit to Ireland. When the older woman went to look for the young girl she couldn't find her anywhere. She had disappeared without a trace and left no message. She was never heard of again.

Her father tried every channel open to him – the police, the shipping agents, and every relative, friend, or former neighbour he knew in America. A search was made, inquiries were pursued, every lead or half-lead was followed, but the girl was never found. Family tradition had it that it was then her father swore that no other child of his would ever emigrate to America again as long as he lived. And that, apparently, was how one of his younger daughters came to have a match made for her with a man from the little island of Innishturk.

'Better Innishturk than white slavery in New Orleans or San Francisco,' a neighbour, home on holidays from Chicago, was reported to have said, when he heard about the marriage.

A few days later, my mother sent me to the well for a can of spring water. The well was only a stone's throw from the sea, so I did a detour. I hid the can behind a clump of rushes in a corner of the well-field and went down to the shore. First I started looking for shells, the little white conch-shaped ones we called butter-rolls. My friends, Mau Glynn and Geraldine

Dunne, and I used to collect them because they were tiny and pretty and generally hard to find. A Royal Air Force pilot had told us that this kind of shell – but a much bigger, smoother, shinier version of it – was used instead of money by the Maldivian islanders when he was stationed in the Far East during the war.

The tide was on its way in, so when I could find no more butter-rolls I went to have a look at the shrimps and cobblers in the big rockpool. After that, I skimmed a few flat stones across the water and then sat on a high rock to watch the tide coming in. I loved the fine spray the waves threw up when they hit the jags of the big black rock opposite me and then flowed down over its sides like ragged lace curtains that instantly disappeared. The spray was like a fine cool shower on my face and arms, but I was careful not to let it really wet me in case my mother might realise I had gone down to the shore.

Soon the tide came swirling in around the big rock where I was sitting and began to fill up the little inlet below me. I listened for the hollow sucking sound the waves made as they drew back and got ready for another run up the strand. The beach was only a few hundred yards from our house, and it was as much a part of my life, growing up, as the yard, the road, my father's fields, and the big green mound called Fairy Hill where we spent our time climbing and playing. The little town of Louisburgh was about a quarter of a mile away on the other side, but when the weather was fine the beach was always where we wanted to play.

I loved the sea on calm sunny evenings like this one. But often, without much warning, it could turn rough and stormy. When a great winter gale blew in from the Atlantic, we both loved it and were terrified by it. Sometimes those wild, high-gusting rainstorms lashed the coast for days on end. Lying in bed in the back-room at night, watching the beam of the old

Clare Island lighthouse sweeping across the bedroom wall, listening to the wind howling in the chimney, and the heavy surf pounding on the beach below Tony Durkan's bank, gave me one of the sensations I loved best in all the world – the feeling of being safe and warm in a world full of noise and danger.

But even on fine days there were certain moments when I was terrified by the sea too. My worst nightmares had to do with times during the summer holidays when there was a low tide and we had to go down to the shore together to pick carrageen. We harvested and sold carrageen moss during the 1940s because the income from our small farm wasn't enough to feed and educate nine of us. My mother was a quick and expert carrageen picker, but she often went out very far to fill her bag. The thickest bunches grew on submerged rocks away out beyond the low-water level, and I was terrified that a big wave might come suddenly and sweep her off her feet, especially when she was alone and nearly out of her depth. I was afraid that the heavy bag might overbalance her on those slippery rocks, and she might be drowned before anyone could reach the spot in time to save her. The very worst of my nightmares had to do with those carrageen-picking days, especially if a heavy swell came on and the currents suddenly turned strong and dangerous.

So the sea brought me secret fears and nightmares. But it also brought me hopes of adventure and dreams. This evening as I watched the tide coming in and saw the sun sinking slowly into the dazzling watery gap between Clare Island and Achill, I began to think again about those men from Mayo who went to Patagonia looking for gold. I thought about the neighbour who died in Buenos Aires and wondered how he managed to get from Bunowen to Tierra del Fuego if it was such a long journey. I wondered what strange places he might have seen along the way. I didn't know enough geography yet to invent itineraries for him. That would come later.

As I was sitting on my high rock looking out across Clew Bay at the sun setting near the old lighthouse on Clare Island that evening, an exciting thought came to me suddenly. I saw the wide glittering path of the sun across the surface of the sea in a new way. It seemed, for a few minutes, to be like a real path, one that you could follow or take directions by. There it was, bright and clear like a gleaming golden causeway that stretched all the way from the edge of the rock where I was sitting to the exact spot where the sun would soon touch the rim of the horizon.

I decided then that the best way to get to Patagonia would be to follow the path of the sun, to steer straight along on top of it or beside it, in a ship. Yes, I'd need a ship. A galleon, a schooner or a clipper maybe, but any kind of a ship would do me, and if I kept going straight out there over the horizon and followed the path of the sun into the west, then one day I'd surely arrive at Patagonia.

A few minutes later the sun dipped down over the rim of the ocean, the glittering path vanished from the surface of the sea, and the water around the edges of the rocks began to turn black and cold. The rising tide looked different now. It seemed dark and choppy all of a sudden, even though there was still a golden glow in the western sky where the sun had set. But the water was nearly inky-black now under the rock where I was sitting.

I hurried back to the well, filled my can with water, and went off home as fast as I could. I had a handful of small, finely-ridged seashells in my pocket. As I turned them over between my fingers I stood for a minute at the crossroads looking across the fields towards my friend Mau's house, and then I made myself a promise, 'Some day I'll follow the path of the sun and I'll keep going until I get to Tierra del Fuego.'

3

TO THE ANDES

If Valparaíso didn't originally figure in my dreams of voyaging to faraway places, that was only because I hadn't heard of it yet. I probably came across the name for the first time when I was in fifth or sixth class in the primary school. It was the title of a little poem in one of our Irish reading books:

> Tháinig long ó Valparaíso,
> Scaoileadh téad a seol sa chuan.
> Chuir a h-ainm dom í gcuimhne
> Ríocht na gréine, tír na mbua.

Being an *aficionado* of all things nautical and exotic, I thought occasionally about the ship in that poem, a sailing-vessel that dropped anchor in some unnamed Irish harbour a great many years ago when tall-masted ships still crossed the ocean under billowing white sails. The exotic angle was where she had come from, a seaport called Valparaíso on the coast of Chile on the Pacific coast of South America.

Oliver Saint John Gogarty had composed the poem in its original English version and called it 'The Ship.' It was a wishful run of rhymed quatrains about the call of the sea, and the lure of distant places like Valparaíso which the poet refers to as 'a white umbrageous city' set under the blue slopes of the Andes. Gogarty, a well-known figure in Dublin literary life around the turn of the century, appears in the opening section of James Joyce's *Ulysses* as 'stately plump Buck Mulligan.'

But the poem I learned in school was not 'The Ship' in that original English version composed by Oliver Saint John Gogarty. I didn't have to wrestle with odd ideas like an 'umbrageous city' or 'the night-empurpled deep,' which seem to me now to spoil the simplicity of the verses. A felicitous little Irish translation had been made by a Gaelic scholar called Pádraig de Brún, and that was the poem that generations of Irish children like myself learned in school.

Decades later, unable to find a copy of Gogarty's original, I made a loose English version of the poem for myself, working from Pádraig de Brún's little Irish lyric. This is how it turned out:

> Once a ship from Valparaíso
> Dropped its anchor in the bay,
> Etching in my heart a vision
> Of a kingdom far away,
>
> Calling to a distant journey
> Out beyond cold cloud and mist
> Where below the blue-sloped Andes
> Glistening coastlands westwards sit.
>
> But I was young and wouldn't listen.
> Other visions filled my heart,
> Hopes, ambitions, life before me,
> Dreams that poems and tales impart.
>
> Long ago the ship departed
> Westward with its mast of gold,
> Wrote its legend on night's parchment
> Where the trackless stars glow cold.
>
> Come again strange ship I pray you.
> Gleam white city by the sea.
> By your great Pacific reaches
> Let my life's fulfilment be.

I had taken liberties with the text, especially in the final verse. But the result, although it was neither accurate nor, strictly-speaking, poetic, served a personal purpose which was important to me at the time. It was a period in my life when I felt very much in the doldrums and had practically given up all hope of ever seeing such far-off places as Valparaíso or Tierra del Fuego. Translating the poem helped me to keep faith with the fading dreams of my childhood, at least in terms of Czeslaw Milosz's dictum that 'what's uttered strengthens itself'.

I couldn't say exactly when it was that those childhood dreams about Patagonia and Tierra del Fuego had begun to recede into some less-visited corner of my mind and eventually dropped out of active consciousness altogether. Probably during the 1950s, by which time I had gone away to boarding school and left the Atlantic coast behind me for a small Irish-language college on the shores of Lough Mask in a more inland part of County Mayo. This lake, full of boggy brown water with a porous limestone bed, had a reputation among freshwater anglers as a good trout and salmon fishing place, but no other claim to fame that I knew of.

There were definitely no graceful ships or picturesque ports, no wrecks of old Spanish galleons or mysterious treasures to be found – or even imagined – in the environs of Tourmakeady, pleasant little watering-place though it was. And even I, with my propensity for romantic dreaming, knew that the only navigational excitements I was ever likely to see there would be the little boats that took anglers out fishing when the May-fly rose, or the silent circlings of small craft on calm cloudy evenings when they hoped the trout might bite.

I was learning history now, and had read the story of a Norman knight called de Burgo whose lands were situated somewhere in the neighbourhood of the lake. He got rid of one of his enemies – who was probably also his kinsman – by drowning him in the lake, roped to a sackful of stones. The New York gangster Dutch Schultz used a variation of the same method when he set a disobedient henchman's feet in a bucket of cement before consigning him to the waters of Manhattan harbour. Gory deeds, but committed in locations with which I had some kind of notional familiarity.

The comparative advantage enjoyed by places like Tierra del Fuego and Valparaíso – in my mind at least – was that they were far enough away for me to know practically nothing about their ordinary life or the dark deeds that might be committed by their shadier inhabitants. I hadn't lived in a town of any size yet, much less in a big city, and I had grown up in that half of the twentieth century when Ireland was still a country with a strong rural flavour, and not yet marked much by the sophistications of urban life.

That was to change for me at the age of seventeen when I went to Dublin and enrolled as a student in Carysfort College on the southern outskirts of the capital. It was the beginning of a gradual growing away from the things of my childhood and the Atlantic seaboard, where my dreams of Tierra del Fuego and Patagonia had been nurtured, but it wasn't altogether a growing away from the sea. In fact, whenever I remember the first night I spent in Carysfort, the sound that comes most clearly to my mind is the haunting repetitive wail of a foghorn – unfamiliar to me then – in the hush of a sleeping dormitory on a September night.

On that far-off day in autumn 1954 when I arrived in Blackrock to start training as a teacher, my life began to follow a path that didn't look as if it would ever lead me anywhere near Patagonia or Tierra del Fuego. My childhood dreams were well behind me now. It was the 1950s in Ireland, a post-war decade of limited opportunities and restricted horizons. In 1956 I qualified as a teacher and found a job in a big primary school in west-central Dublin.

But I was a dreamer of sorts, still, though my thoughts now were turning to more intangible horizons, the transcendental yearnings and idealistic strivings of a youthful religious vocation. In September 1956 I joined the community of the Sisters of Mercy in Carysfort, and committed myself to a life that had 'a quest for God and spiritual perfection' as its personal goal, and the austerely-practical purpose of 'serving the poor, sick, and ignorant' as its communal project.

The latter phrase had been put into currency in the early nineteenth century by a certain Bishop Murphy of Cork, but in the Ireland of the 1950s it still pointed, however infelicitously, to a field of human need that was visible and distressing and hard to ignore. It was a panorama of poverty that called for widespread voluntary as well as state effort to eradicate its worst ills. The community I joined had been building hospitals and schools, training nurses and teachers, and providing informal social services on a voluntary basis for well over a century. Communities of women called Sisters of Mercy had been working away quietly and steadily, opening up paths to better educational and social opportunities for young people from the needier sections of Irish society, since the first small group of Mercy women came together in Baggot Street in Dublin in the early 1830s.

Social and economic prospects for the great majority of young people in Ireland in the 1950s were, to say the least of it, restricted. It was a decade of grey poverty, discouraging employment statistics, and high levels of emigration. So it would have been difficult to foresee that, within a few decades, the country would have made sufficient economic progress for the state to be able to finance fully the educational, social and health services that up to then had depended heavily on inputs in voluntary service and capital from socially-committed groups like the Sisters of Mercy.

When I started work as a fledgling teacher in Dublin in the 1950s, the struggle against poverty, particularly in poor areas of the city, was an uphill haul where basic resources were scarce, and progress was so slow as to be almost invisible. You wondered if anything would ever change. But a couple of decades later – by which time I had taught in three city schools, studied by night in the university, worked with student-teachers in Carysfort, and spent five years running a small secondary school in North County Dublin – there were perceptible signs of social change.

The 1970s brought a more economically-buoyant and socially-conscious era not just to Ireland but to most of the countries across the developed world as well. Europe had emerged from its post-war era of struggle and austerity. Ireland had begun to slough off the old skin of poverty. A concern for social justice, with worldwide as well as national and local perspectives, was in the air. That was when I began to think seriously about going to work in one of the underdeveloped countries in what was then known as the Third World.

Kenya was on my horizons because the Mercy community had been running schools and hospitals there since the middle of the 1950s, and my sister Sarah was working as a missionary in neighbouring Uganda. But South America was in my thoughts too, not because I was dreaming of Patagonia or Tierra del Fuego anymore – I think I had forgotten all about them – but because the call of that continent reached many religious communities in the '60s and '70s after Pope John XXIII made a moving plea on behalf of its poor people, millions of whom were living wretchedly under one form or another of dictatorship.

In the early 1970s I was working in Saint Joseph's Secondary School in Rush in North County Dublin. Some of the worst news at the time had been coming to us from the embattled and bitterly divided-communities less than a hundred miles away from us to the north – after Internment Without Trial was summarily imposed in Northern Ireland. But in September 1973 Chile erupted violently into the news too, and it was the worst kind of news. A right-wing military dictatorship had bloodily overthrown the precarious governing coalition led by the country's socialist president Salvador Allende. General Augusto Pinochet, leading a junta of hard men, the commanders of the country's armed forces, had violently seized power. Painful experiences were to follow, and a long dark night – which nobody dreamed would last for sixteen years – had begun for the people of Chile.

A regime of repression, fear, censorship, and state-organised abuse of human rights was imposed on the population, or at least on that wide and vulnerable section of it that differed in political outlook, social rank and economic conditions from Pinochet and the historically-privileged minority in Chilean society who supported him. In Rush, I was reading the educational and social-justice texts of Paolo Freire and Helder Camara, and South America was emerging more and more clearly on my horizons. My readings were coming from Brazil, but the pull on my heart was towards Chile.

And then, in 1974, my life took an unlooked-for turn. In September of that year I was appointed president of Carysfort College in Blackrock where I had qualified as a teacher in the 1950s and worked as a junior lecturer during the 1960s. It had been in a state of institutional slumber for decades, and then, with the passing of its long-term Victorian-style president of thirty years, had run into a period of acute crisis and student turbulence. Two presidents had tried without success to deal with the situation on a gradualist basis. But by 1974 it was clear that a root-and-branch reform was needed in the college and that it would have to be carried into effect in an urgent and systematic way. So instead of a ticket to the Third World I was given a ride back to Carysfort, and a seat behind the long black-topped desk in the president's office. I had deeply conflicting feelings about the assignment.

I accepted the challenge of the Carysfort presidency with a very reluctant heart – not because I didn't want to see the necessary reforms carried through, and the educational and professional work of the college made as responsive as possible to the needs and purposes of Irish society, but because my South American project would have to be put on hold, indefinitely. There was no saying when I might be able to think about it as a realistic prospect again.

So I felt stymied. The day I had my first meeting with the academic staff in Carysfort in September 1974, I remember surprising even myself by confiding to the Registrar, whom I barely knew at the time, that while I'd be doing my very best for the college my real aim was to get to South America as soon as I could. I can still remember the expression on his otherwise impeccably-guarded features as he digested that oddly-timed bit of information.

Carysfort turned out, as time went on, to be a challenging and engaging experience for me. But challenges and engagements don't last forever. Life moves on. I was sitting behind my desk in the president's office there one autumn evening in 1982 and feeling more acutely than usual the restlessness of middle-life. I was forty-five, had useful work to do, and didn't lack for demanding occupations. The college was a busy national centre for training teachers, and there were projects and problems enough to keep me on stretch for seven days of the week if I wanted it that way. But still I was restless.

When I had come back to Carysfort in 1974, the college

urgently needed a programme of expansion and modernisation – a link with the university, extra funding, new courses, more staff, academic and administrative reforms, and an extensive programme of building and re-adaptation. So, in spite of my initial disappointment about being assigned to South Dublin instead of South America, my energies rallied to the demands of the situation, and by degrees I became thoroughly involved in the work. It was a good time to be in teacher education. There was scope for change and innovation. There were stimulating ideas in the air, and good people around who were willing to put their energies behind them.

But eight years later, in 1982, the link with the university was consolidated, the building programme was finished, the main reforms had been carried through, new courses were being taught and others were on the drafting board – and I was feeling restless. Two years earlier, the poet Seamus Heaney had finished five years in the college's English Department and had left to take up an appointment in Harvard. I used to think sometimes about the image he used to explain to me, thoughtfully as was his wont, that the time had come for him to move on. It was an image that might have come from a dream. The tent he had pitched when he came to Carysfort in 1975 – the notion was of a capacious Bedouin affair located somewhere along the edge of a desert – had been propped up against the side of a ship on some famous waterway. The Suez Canal or even the Red Sea came to mind. But now the ship had begun to move away, and so must he. His journey was to take him into auspicious waters, to Nobel honours and world stature as a poet.

The image of that departing ship came back to me afterwards. I had been aware for years of a growing inner restlessness. In the 1980s it began to take the form of an involuntary distancing from the life and concerns around me, especially when they wore a public face. This mixture of restlessness and inner detachment had been gaining on me as time went by, and it wasn't amenable to being appeased either by extra work or extra distraction. So on this autumn evening in 1982 I found myself sitting in my office after most people had gone home, thinking about South America and the project I had put on hold when I was transferred from Rush to Carysfort in 1974.

The window opposite my desk looked south towards the Dublin mountains. I could see a pair of crows coming and going, circling around the crown of a thinning old pine-tree. Sometimes they made short bursts of flight towards the nearby gable, and then come back again to circle the tree, as if they couldn't make up their minds whether to roost in the window-slit of the old Victorian building or not.

Beyond the long line of red-brick buildings, I could see the grey Georgian home, the nucleus around which the big Carysfort complex had gradually come into being. Beside the Georgian mansion and all around it stretched the broad green acres of Carysfort Park. There were formal gardens, terraced flowerbeds, small copses of beech, oak, chestnut, lime and sycamore, a walled kitchen garden, an orchard, stables, old coach-houses, and, in the dip of a gently-sloping lawn, the ornamental pond we called 'the lake.' Beyond that again were cornfields, meadows, and soft green pastures where cattle grazed. Behind my back, out of sight of the office where I was sitting, were the new buildings that had just been completed and the more recently landscaped areas of the college grounds.

All this pleasant spreading South Dublin greensward, I understood, had once been the deer-park of the great Allen estate which had stretched across wide areas of counties Dublin and Wicklow at the beginning of the eighteenth century. This beautiful parkland had become part of the marriage dowry of a daughter of Baron Allen, who married into the English Proby family and brought the Carysfort title to this part of Ireland during the same century. It was without doubt a pleasant place to work. I had the added privilege of living there too.

So if contentment could come from having a provident community, interesting colleagues, lively students, useful work, and an aesthetically-pleasing and ecologically-privileged environment, I should have had it, and in abundance. But I hadn't. Not altogether. South America and Chile had begun to flicker on the rim of my horizon again and were feeding some inner flame of need or restlessness. I hadn't forgotten about Chile in the eight years since I left Rush, but this evening I realised that the time had come to put the pressure of reality on what, up to then, had been mainly wishful thinking. I intended to apply for sabbatical leave the following year, and Chile was where I wanted to spend it. I'd have to make contact with somebody who was working in a poor region in Santiago.

But the problem, as I quickly realised sitting there in an office where I could usually get things done with a certain amount of despatch, often just by lifting the telephone, was that I didn't know a single person in South America, much less in Chile, on that date near the end of 1982. So I had to take the problem to bed with me, unsolved, and that night, somewhere in the drifting-off period between waking and sleeping, I found the beginnings of an answer. I remembered that Mary Connaughton, with whom I had taught in Goldenbridge many years before, had told me once that her brother Alo was working as a Columban missionary in Chile. I rang her the next morning and asked for his address, and if possible a telephone number. She told me she'd look up the telephone number and call me back.

When she rang me later in the day, I wrote the address and phone number carefully on a sheet of office memo-paper, put down the telephone and sat back in my chair, very pleased to have located my first personal contact in South America – and not just in South America but in Santiago, the capital of Chile. Alo Connaughton, I discovered afterwards, was the Regional Director of the Columban Fathers in South America. My project looked set to prosper.

But then a curious thing happened. A mute resistance took over inside me, an obstinate refusal to move, act, or even think directly about making that first contact with Chile. This lasted for several months. I didn't want to lift the telephone, take up my pen, or even read or talk or think about South America anymore. It was a passive state, an unformulated refusal to budge rather than a reasoned rejection or even an outright burst of negative energy, and so, of course, it was all the harder to deal with.

Soon I began letting myself have bleak thoughts about how far away Chile was, the difficulties of learning a new language, the repressive political regime in Santiago and the danger of living in a country ruled by somebody like General Pinochet – not to mention the fact that Chile was a country prone to earthquakes. I folded the little sheet of memo-paper with the Santiago address into a very small square, and stuck it under the container for pens and pencils on a corner of my desk, and there it stayed, a silent but vaguely radioactive presence, for five or six months.

As time went on, I'd take it out occasionally, look at the address, and think about writing a letter to Alo Connaughton, but then I'd lose courage and put the bit of paper back in its place again without having done anything practical about it. One day I got as far as picking up the telephone and dialling the number of the Columban House in Santiago. But the thought of that unknown country on the other side of the world, and the possibility that somebody might answer my phonecall with a barrage of rapid Spanish was too much for me. I didn't make the telephone call either.

The cluttered familiarity of my office desk in Carysfort seemed strangely comforting to me at those moments. The mail, memos, minutes of board meetings, documents about staff appointments and salary negotiations, the discussions, plans, and development projects, all the small change of my day-to-day life and work in the college, maybe it had some hold on me after all? Even if it was only the hold of things that were familiar and accustomed? I didn't like to think so, but, as my old friend Sister Nathy used to say, facts are stubborn things. It remained to be seen whether my desire to get to South America was as stubborn as the mundane and entangling facts that bound me to the office desk and my familiar routines in Carysfort.

It was only when Alo Connaughton came home to Ireland on holidays a few months later, that I finally overcame my resistance and eventually made contact with him about trying to find a place to spend a period of sabbatical leave in Chile. He came to lunch in Carysfort one day, fresh from a morning's work on his father's farm in County Westmeath. The thought of that farm helped me, somehow. I asked him about the possibility of finding a place where I could spend some time with a community working in a poor *población* in Santiago. In my private thoughts I saw this as a timid testing of unknown waters with my big toe. I had lived for years in privileged and secure surroundings. I didn't know how I'd manage with urban struggle and poverty in a distant and unfamiliar country.

Alo, quiet man of action and excellent friend that he turned out to be, made no fuss about finding me a place. He put me in contact with the Columban Sisters and the Cross and Passion community, both of whom had houses in poor areas on the outskirts of Santiago. He also advised me to spend the first couple of months of my leave, be it long or short, in Cochabamba at the Maryknoll Language Institute. Without a basic knowledge of Spanish – he didn't put the matter so bluntly but I got the message – I might as well stay at home. It was good advice, even if I didn't relish the prospect of spending any part of my limited sabbatical leave in a language institute, though it did help a little to discover that it was located in the middle of the Bolivian Andes.

After that it was a question of applying for leave and finding ways of easing myself out of the office in Carysfort. This turned out to be a slightly more complicated process than I had bargained for. The main parties involved in releasing me for the rather less than twelve months I had applied for, were the Sisters of Mercy who owned the college, the Archbishop of Dublin who was its manager, and the state Department of Education which paid my salary. None of them had any specific objections to my taking sabbatical leave after nearly ten years on the job, but they all seemed to have some difficulty about my wanting to spend it in a poor población in Santiago. What could that possibly have to do with teacher-training in Carysfort? I was at a loss as to how to give them a convincing answer.

Eventually I got the various clearances I needed. But delays and complications of one kind or another meant that it was the summer of 1984 by the time I was able to pack my bags, hand over the office with its tidied-up files to the College Registrar, and set out on my first long journey to South America.

And what a long journey that first one turned out to be! I had asked the travel agency, Journey Latin America, to find me an economic air ticket, and they took me at my word. The price was low in proportion as the route was tortuous and the weariness-factor high. I might have been starting on a mini world tour. Dublin, London, Amsterdam, Zurich, Caracas, Panama City, Lima, La Paz, Cochabamba – all in the space of about thirty-six hours. Only determination, ignorance, and the dogged enthusiasm of a first-timer – an escapee from desk work and a lifetime of religious discipline and routine – kept me going. I was keeping a verse-journal at the time, and it catches the flavour of things in its own way:

> Airport lounges,
> transit camps
> briefly incarcerating
> on miles of antiseptic terrazzo,
> the checked-in, waved-out plane-loads,
> skybound for elsewhere.

I was heartily sick of airports, airline food, stale transit-lounges, hot airless nights, times that kept changing over invisible longitude-lines, and just about everything to do with long-distance travel by the time I got to my destination. I had a stopover for a few hours in Lima. The parts of the city that I saw, mainly its wretched *pueblos jovenes* – the shanty-towns that were still mushrooming around the periphery of the faded old colonial capital – produced a dispiriting reflection:

> The Incas' revenge,
> sandy streets of a desert city,
> unpaved, unfinished, unending,
> climbing steep stony hills,
> grey, stark, unbeautiful,
> under heavy tilting skies,
> a sunless noonday
> too close for comfort,
> the reversal of all my known Julys.

La Paz was different. It had the thin unfamiliar air of a city holding its breath up near the cold roof-ridge of the world. I had been told that oxygen masks had been known to drop inside aircraft cabins when the doors were opened at the end of a flight, because, at that altitude, the ordinary air outside could be lower in oxygen than the controlled atmosphere of the cabin. I never witnessed the phenomenon myself, but I felt the thin strangeness of the air that first night as I stepped out onto the tarmac. In my journal I wrote:

> La Paz,
> plunging city
> hanging off the flat roof of the earth.
> Thin rarefied air,
> brief, strange stopover.
> Splendour and squalor
> under the brooding snows
> of shadowy Illimani.

My immediate destination was Cochabamba, a sprawling dusty city in an upland valley of the Bolivian Andes. It was an old Spanish colonial city which had come into being around the activities of silver mining and agriculture. There were vestiges of eighteenth-century architecture and a certain period-graciousness about the old civic and ecclesiastical buildings in the centre of the city. But, in general, there was a depressing contrast between the poverty and hand-to-mouth squalor of the overcrowded man-made city environment, and the natural beauty of the landscape around it. A high ring of blue mountains encircled the city and, because it was winter, they often showed ragged snowy peaks. I found this a wonderful relief from the dirt and stench of the city's open markets and the alternating mud and dust of its unpaved streets.

I was weary beyond words when I arrived in Cochabamba on the evening of 5 July, 1984, two days, but many worlds, away from the soft summer lawns of Carysfort. My first note about the city was brief as I tried to keep in check uneasy feelings of dislocation and loneliness:

> Cochabamba,
> sprawling city
> winking in the warm darkness
> of an unfamiliar night.
> Dusty shops and bars
> glimmering under dim streetlights.
> Odour of palm trees and eucalyptus,
> intimate sense of distance and loneliness,
> irretrievably far from all that I knew.

Before I fell asleep that night, a fog of lonely, panicky thoughts closed in around me. 'Here I am,' I thought bleakly, 'in the middle of the Andes, in the middle of South America, in the middle of Bolivia, in the middle of a strange dusty city thousands of feet above the sea, in the middle of a country that hasn't even an outlet to the sea, in the middle of a vast continent where I only know one person – and he's miles away in Santiago, and I can't even speak the language, and if I wanted to get out now I couldn't... I'd be too weary even to think about how to make my way out of here...' I fell asleep at last, out of sheer merciful exhaustion.

After that came the intimate travails of life in a language school. I had enrolled for a six-week Spanish course, and, although I knew it wasn't nearly enough, it was all I felt I could afford out of my eleven months leave from Carysfort. The Institute was run by the North American Maryknoll Missionaries with a staff of Bolivian language teachers. The atmosphere was easy and friendly, and the place itself was like a well-watered oasis in the middle of a sprawling urban wilderness of dust and poverty. But the process of learning a new language under time pressure was difficult.

I felt every day of my forty-seven years, and something inside me creaked with reluctance every time I climbed the stairs to one of the tiny classrooms where we got intensive, one-to-one, oral-aural instruction from a series of earnest, hard-working teachers. The Institute had an outdoor swimming pool, and, although it was mid-winter, I worked out some of my resistances – and learned by dogged repetition to count in Spanish – threshing my way up and down through its chilly waters. I did a dozen lengths or so every morning before breakfast, straight after I got out of bed at half-past-six. It was a bit of useful Spartan self-discipline – born of my habit of all-year-round swimming at Seapoint in Dublin – that would be quite beyond me a few years later.

Meanwhile, I was getting my first impressions of life in one of the poorest regions of South America. Bolivia was the country to which the great Venezuelan leader, Simon Bolivar, had left his name and his dream of a United States of liberated Latin American countries. It was also the place where Ernesto 'Che' Guevara had more recently tried to spearhead a continent-wide Marxist revolution modelled on his Cuban experience. But in day-to-day reality it was a fairly chaotically-run country with a hand-to-mouth economy that was dogged by runaway inflation. Side by side with showy wealth – derived it was said from the lucrative narcotics business – some of the oldest and most unchanging Andean cultures still survived, and with them an ancient stony poverty.

In my journal I tried in vain to convey the impact this strange city and country had on me:

> I walked brown streets, dusty and stony
> where drains trickled darkly across parched pathways,
> and babies splashed while mothers washed clothes
> in muddy canal-runlets, to the hum of flies.

A black pig snuffled through rank weeds
along a dusty scrub-bank, and lean grey sheep,
suckled by mud-coloured lambs, nosed up to the very
gates of rich houses for scarce weedy pasture.
Mass was the same, in a different language,
with duskier skins, darker eyes, broader faces.
Outside the church, street-vendors counted
devalued pesos into limp bundles under drooping trees.
They sold olives, peanuts, sweets and thin ice-cream.
An unfamiliar piping of tree frogs
punctuated the warm windy twilight.
A high wind swayed the palm trees
and the drooping eucalyptus boughs.
It dropped into stillness suddenly,
clearing the night for a ringed moon
of shimmering brightness
and the insistent rhythmic beat
of Andean fiesta music.

For Bolivia's national holiday at the beginning of August we got a week off from language school, and a group of us set out to visit Cuzco, the old Inca capital in upland Peru. Our journey would take us from Cochabamba to La Paz, across the Altiplano as far as Lake Titicaca, over the lake at the Tiquina Straits, across the border into Peru, and then on through the mountains to Puno, and after that to Cuzco and finally up to the peaks of Machu Picchu – and then back. It turned out to be a raw experience.

We stayed overnight in La Paz on our way up to the lake. My morning swims and long walks had kept me fit, so I didn't suffer from the altitude sickness that afflicted some of my travelling companions. But I felt again the strange thinness of the air, the piercing brightness of the stars – they looked as if you could reach up and touch them – and the icy atmosphere of the night when the moon, surrounded by a vivid rainbow-nimbus, seemed to turn the shelving rim of the Altiplano into a vast shadowy precipice.

We reached the lake-shore after a dust-choked ride in a minibus across the brown featureless landscape of the Altiplano. Lake Titicaca, the cradle of various lost and surviving Andean civilisations, was like a vast inland sea. Its dark-blue waters stretched away for miles on every side except where the horizon was broken by rugged lilac-grey mountains and jagged, skellig-like rock formations along the shore. We passed tiny scattered villages, huddles of brown adobe houses raggedly fringed with dusty eucalyptus trees. Around solitary windowless mud cabins we saw brown pigs and scratching fowl, while lean bony cattle and goats tried to graze pastures where not a single blade of grass was to be seen. Heaps of stones, roughly scooped together, made makeshift pathways to the edge of the lake. The women were the only bright spots on the horizon. They caught my eye again and again as we travelled across that endless dusty plain:

> And always, like spots of woven brightness
> on a tapestry of grey-brown earth
> the wide-skirted, derby-hatted, burdened
> Indian women, trekking with bright bultos –
> vividly-patterned woven blankets –
> wrapped around goods and babies.
> They trudged along roadsides,
> crossed stony terraced fields,
> climbed endless desolate hills,
> toiling towards the pueblo, the market,
> the crowded convivial lakeside fiesta
> the rhythmic drumbeat of communal celebration.

In the early afternoon we crossed the lake over the brown churning waters at Tiquina Straits, and, after another long dusty ride through the mountains, arrived at a lakeside *pueblo* called Copacabana where a religious festival was in progress. Here the narrow streets were filled to overflowing with people: soldiers, tailors, cooks, conjurers, folk-dancers, policemen, country people. They were buying goods of every conceivable kind: fish, meat, herbs, huge sausages, bright plastic flowers, toys, statues, hats, buckets, baskets, native crafts of all sorts, especially the impressively-patterned woven bags and colourful blankets which flash vividly across the screen of my memory whenever I think about Bolivia.

Newly out from Europe, I found it hard to stomach some of the sights and smells and raw sensations of that overcrowded fiesta by the lakeside. The open latrines, heat, dirt, excrement, sweat, rank smells of food and cooking – all the dense detritus of otherwise scattered lives, lived in isolation among distant hills, was now packed tightly for those few days into a tiny town on the edge of the lake, until it seemed the place could hold no more. I knew I'd have to toughen up if I ever wanted to live or work in this part of South America. I hoped, and in my heart I prayed, that Chile might be different.

A long, crowded train journey – we had to spend more than three hours just queuing for the tickets – brought us from Puno on the edge of Lake Titicaca up to Cuzco, the old Inca valley of sunlight, fertility and mystery in the heart of the Peruvian highlands. In this city, for the first time since I arrived in South America, I felt like a tourist and was uncomfortable. The former Inca capital was a mixture of stony remains of pre-Colombian fortresses, temple-ruins, ornate Spanish colonial churches, huge sombre convents and monasteries, hostelries and eateries of all kinds, narrow lanes and wide, untidy street-markets. Deep pockets of squalor and poverty lurked behind the historic façades at almost every point. In my notebook I wrote:

> City of light and temples,
> fertile elevated valley
> where a thousand shafts of sunlight
> play on vast stone-cut fortresses,
> massive geometric symbols
> of a sun-worshipping people.
> City of Spanish churches,
> monastery-museums, tall portals,
> iron-studded doors, obscure winding cloisters,
> dank bone-houses, ornate forgotten tombs
> of *conquistadores* who raised their swords
> and jewelled crosses in pitiless dominance
> over enslaved peoples.
> City of tourists and Diner's cards,
> profuse untidy dirty street markets,
> piercing cold of nights and mornings,
> shimmering suns at noonday.
> Your stone is remote, forbidding,
> unaccommodating to flesh and blood.
> Your beauty is still the fertile valley,
> the temple of your shining god, the sun
> poured in at daybreak over silent hills,
> warming all life to brightness,
> perplexing with might-have-beens
> the transient tourist memory.

Machu Picchu, the so-called secret city of the Incas, was a labyrinth of massive mountain-top ruins. Hidden away on its terraced heights amid scenery of breathtaking loveliness, it had all the mystery of an enigmatic deserted shrine, the privileged retreat of a chosen caste maybe, or an elite esoteric place of worship. But the ruins weren't, in the end, the thing that impressed me most about Machu Picchu. It was the unexpected sub-tropical lushness of the vegetation in the mountain chasms plunging away below us that really held my eye, and the startling contrasts of light and colour, the shadows chasing one another through deep crevasses and verdant wooded valleys. The unexpected richness of that densely-forested landscape miles below us was far more wonderful to me – because it was full of a vivid, ongoing natural life – than the massive, puzzling deserted ruins on the mountain top.

What I remembered about Machu Picchu afterwards was that it rained heavily when the bus took us down again to the railway station. It was the first rain I had seen since I left Ireland, and I felt a surge of welcome for it after the parching dust of Bolivia, until I saw the ragged children of the food vendors and souvenir sellers taking shelter from the downpour under the carriages of the train. I almost trod on a baby wrapped in rags lying on the damp ground under the wheel of our carriage as I was climbing in. Again I saw myself as a tourist and felt uncomfortable. There might not be any aristocratic warrior-Incas or haughty Spanish *conquistadores* in this part of the world anymore, but there were still people of privilege, like us, and ragged unfortunate fellow human beings who weren't much better off yet than shivering slaves.

It was piercingly cold on the late-evening train that took us back to Cuzco. By the time we got into the city I wondered if any part of me would ever feel warm or ordinary again. The same intense shivering cold was still in my bones when I got back to the Language Institute in Cochabamba a few days later. I had to take to my bed with a heavy feverish flu, complicated by a bout of the embarrassing affliction that fellow students called the Inca quickstep. We had been warned about the food and water, but you can't live indefinitely out of a rucksack.

Back at the Institute I realised I had got off lightly. Four of the men had come down with hepatitis. It was a mid-term break that, for one reason or another, most of us would be unlikely to forget.

4

TO CHILE

Six weeks in language school in Bolivia was all I had allowed for, and, as things turned out, just about the limit of what I could take. My learning powers went on a go-slow after I got back from Cuzco. I was weary of sitting at a desk in a tiny classroom, eyeball to eyeball with one dutiful, serious, brown-eyed Bolivian teacher after another. I was even wearier of finding myself stumbling hopelessly each day over verbs and phrases I felt sure I had mastered, once and for all, the day before.

I was staying with the Guzman family in Cala Cala during those final weeks. They were kind and thoughtful, and unfailingly helpful and encouraging, in spite of the communication problems caused by my doubtful Spanish, but I had reached a learning plateau of some kind. I couldn't absorb any more and, besides, I was more and more anxious to get down to Chile. I had booked my flight to Santiago for 4 September, the first date I could travel after our language classes ended.

This turned out to be a day of general strike and public protest in Chile where people were beginning to take to the streets to show their opposition to the long-standing oppressions of the Pinochet regime. In Bolivia, some of the old hands warned me that things could turn dangerous when there were street protests in Santiago, and they urged me to postpone my flight. But I couldn't bring myself to put it back even for a few days. So, on 4 September, I left Cochabamba for La Paz, and then boarded a Lloyd Aereo Boliviano international flight for Chile.

Alo Connaughton met me at the airport in Santiago. It was good to see his reassuring features and quiet smile again.

'We'll have to go carefully here,' he said after we left the airport and turned off the main road in the direction of the Columban Sisters' house in Neptuno, where we were invited for lunch. This was in the district of Pudahuel, a big *población* on the west side of the city.

'There could be *miguelitos* on some of these streets today,' Alo said.

'What are *miguelitos*?' I asked him.

They were bent nails, twisted into sharp crooked little clusters, an ingenious homemade device to puncture tyres and slow down the big police vehicles that often came roaring into the poor neighbourhoods to intimidate people in times of public protest.

Chile was a sad, smouldering country in September 1984. In the eleven years since General Pinochet and the armed forces had seized power, the hold of the dictatorship over the country seemed to have tightened into an unbreakable grip. The regime's response to the gathering waves of public protest was another campaign of violent repression. You could read the fear and sadness in people's faces – on the sidewalks, on the metro, in the buses – wherever you caught an expression that was off-guard or in repose.

On my first night in Santiago, a boy of fourteen, who was mildly mentally-handicapped, was shot dead by the police on his way home from a protest bonfire. This happened just two blocks down the street from where I was staying with the Columban Sisters in Santa Elena, a poor neighbourhood on the southern outskirts of the city. The state-censored newspapers reported the incident afterwards: the police in the course of their duty had fired at a dangerous extremist.

On the same night, a French missionary priest was shot dead in the bedroom of his little wooden house in the *población* of La Victoria, the victim of another trigger-happy police patrol. So the first two public events I attended after my arrival in Santiago were funerals. One was a sad, angry, helpless local expression of sorrow and sympathy at the burial of the fourteen-year-old boy who was killed near Santa Elena.

The other was a more high-profile event, a public funeral which attracted a certain international media interest because the priest, Padre Andres Jarlan, was a Frenchman. There was barely room to move in or around the big cathedral in the Plaza de Armas in central Santiago that day, not least because the gathering was ringed around with a bristling barrier of heavily-armoured military and police vehicles. And so I got my first taste of the fear and violence that can go with living under a repressive military dictatorship.

Life in Chile, as I first experienced it in that sabbatical year of 1984-85, had a sombre and uneasy feeling sometimes. The poor *poblaciónes*, sprawling areas of densely-populated misery on the edges of the city, were full of fear, resentment and suppressed violence. Underlying the anger against the dictatorship was the age-old and apparently unavailing struggle against a poverty that, in those particular areas, was widespread and crushing. And yet, in some odd, almost contradictory way, I felt at home in Chile practically from the moment I arrived there.

Small familiar things helped, like the warm welcome the Columban Sisters had waiting for me in their little house in Santa Elena. After nearly two months in the brown dust of Bolivia, there was an unexpected pleasure in finding daffodils growing in a garden, and enjoying the beauty of one single graceful nodding bloom in a vase on the table in my tiny bedroom. September is one of the loveliest months in central Chile. It brings the vivid colours and mild temperatures of spring to the fertile valleys around the capital. Whole stretches of the countryside suddenly come to life with a snowy-pink riot of new buds and blossoms, a soft beauty that seems to spread like a frothy spring-tide across the wide acres of almond, peach, apricot and cherry orchards that are a feature of this part of the country. I could feel my spirits rising, even though the first journal entry I made after my arrival in Santiago had its uneasy note:

A single daffodil,
shots in the night,
bonfires of protest hissing
in the grey half-light.
Stoop-shouldered willows
weeping in the cool of spring.
Soft earth of Chile,
nightfall,
I'm at home again.

I didn't know that the shots I heard while I was writing those lines would leave a fourteen-year-old boy dead, just two blocks away from where I was sitting behind windows that were heavily blacked out so as not to attract stray bullets.

Población Santa Elena was a poor, struggling and dismally socially-deprived neighbourhood when I first came to know it in 1984. It was also, after the rains started, a thoroughly muddy and wretched place, a labyrinth of brown streets and narrow lanes full of tiny makeshift houses too flimsy to keep out the cold. In the summer, on the other hand, it was hot and dusty, and the little houses baked like ovens. Unemployment seemed to be the norm rather than the exception, and it was only by small miracles of ingenuity, improvisation, self-help and neighbourly co-operation that many families managed, somehow, to keep going.

The so-called *olla comun,* or common-pot system, was widely used in neighbourhoods like Santa Elena during the years of the Pinochet dictatorship. Operating under the auspices of the church, with help from Caritas Chile, these small collaborative efforts were organised by parish groups, mostly women, who pooled their resources and cooked one meal each day to feed their families. They were a last and humiliating resort against widespread hunger.

Yet even in the poorest neighbourhoods there was one feature of silent beauty that I noticed from the very first morning I stepped out the door in Santa Elena into the narrow muddy street. This was the soaring snowy beauty of the Cordillera on clear spring days. In fine weather people just sat outside their doors to enjoy the vista of the great blue-and-white circle of snow-capped Andes that ringed the city on almost every side. It was a vista that helped to lift people's spirits even if it didn't alleviate their want and hunger. To me as a newcomer it was a constant source of delight and wonder, something to make me forget the brown dust of Cochabamba, and the muddy ruts of the poor streets around us in Santa Elena. I tried to write about it:

> Sunrise,
> the Cordillera gleams
> white, misty-blue.
> Fissures and angles softly merge
> on peaks and slopes.
> This day, still new,
> will bring hunger
> sifting with practised hands
> through refuse-bins.
> In the población
> clean morning light
> hardens and thins.

My sabbatical leave in Chile from September 1984 to June 1985 turned out to be an education in ways that I would have found it hard to explain to my colleagues and the educational authorities back in Ireland. Not just an interval of living among deprivation and poverty, it was also a challenge to reflect on, among other things, the violence of social contrasts. I seldom had reason to visit Santiago's *Barrio Alto*, the upper-class area of the city where life was more luxurious and redolent of taste and wealth than anything I had left behind in Dublin, even in the salubrious environs of Killiney and Foxrock. This historically-entrenched layer of Chilean economic and social privilege was zealously guarded by the forces of the dictatorship who, although they hadn't created it, certainly aspired to enjoy and perpetuate it.

Pairs of commandos in red berets, with machine-guns at the ready, shadowed you every time you went up or down the steps of the Santiago Metro most of that year. In the centre of the city, an armoured truck full of soldiers or police might suddenly pull up in front of you to manhandle and arrest a silent group of men and women with a banner, standing on the side of the street in mute protest against the torture that was regularly used during interrogations at police stations since the earliest days of the dictatorship.

Because there was a rigorous curfew in force all that year, I never really saw or enjoyed the city by night. One of the more recent decrees of the dictatorship had tightened up the censorship and curfew laws because we were supposedly living in 'a state of siege'. This was the regime's response to the unarmed street protests that had recently been gaining support among ordinary citizens. A state of siege was some degrees worse than the regime's eleven-year-old state of emergency. The latter would remain in force for several more years, but the state of siege was lifted the day after I left Chile.

Early in 1985, a further disaster struck the already long-suffering people of central Chile, and for once the military regime was not to blame. A devastating earthquake destroyed large areas along the coast, causing terror, homelessness and extensive damage to property, as well as personal injuries and loss of life. It happened on the Sunday evening of 3 March.

I had come to know and love the small seaport of San Antonio where the Columban Sisters were working at the time. This friendly little town, about a hundred kilometres southwest of Santiago, provided me with access to the ocean and a glorious run of sandy beach with strong surf and a constant, powerful roll of frothing breakers. Within the space of less than two minutes on that evening of 3 March, this little port was shaken to its foundations. Its houses, streets and docks were wrenched from their sockets by a terrible zig-zag earth movement that had its epicentre in the ocean a few miles off the coast to the north. The panic, then and for days afterwards, was recurrent and unnerving. People were afraid that the first big quake would be followed by a tidal wave.

All in all, Chile was a troubled country and, at certain moments, an anxious and uneasy place to live in 1984-85. But for me, paradoxically, it was an experience of life, love and personal liberation. I was magnetised by the country and drawn, not only to its wonderful natural beauty, but even more so to the courage, pain, wry humour and ingenious pragmatism of its poor people. I admired their struggle against poverty and oppression, and was moved by their stubborn hope, which was beaten down, time and again, but which never seemed to die. I wanted to stay in Chile, or if I couldn't stay now, I wanted to come back.

But the days of my sabbatical leave were peeling steadily off the calendar. After the earthquake in March, my few remaining months seemed to be swallowed up in the raw landscape of suffering and misfortune that stretched out on every side of us in the little port of San Antonio. Before the end of June, I was due back behind my desk in Carysfort, a place that seemed as remote to me now as some other planet.

I left Santiago for Dublin on 17 June, 1985. Flying eastwards across the Andes, I began translating a sonnet by Jorge Luis Borges that seemed to mirror my feelings as I said goodbye to South America, and the distance grew between me and the sad, beautiful country of Chile that I had grown to love. The poem began with a question: '*Was there a Garden, or was the Garden a dream?*' That seemed to be my question now too, a sort of wondering doubt in case it might all just turn out to be a fading mirage. With the memory of those months in Chile still alive and vivid inside me, I could identify most closely of all with the poem's ending:

> And yet it is much to have loved,
> To have been happy, to have touched
> The living Garden, even for a day.

Having had such a day, I was reluctant to think that I couldn't have more.

When I got back to Dublin that June I found it almost impossible to settle down to life in Carysfort again. I felt irretrievably distant now from the work I had been doing in Ireland. It was as if an invisible barrier – one that I had no will to remove – separated me from concerns that had once engaged me and seemed pressing and important. This was no longer the vague, unfocussed restlessness I had known in the early 1980s. Rather, it was a clear awareness that I didn't belong here anymore, that there was nothing in Carysfort or in Irish education that others couldn't do with far more conviction and commitment now, than I could.

So, at the end of September 1985, three months after my return, I sat down and wrote a letter to the Mercy Superior General asking to be released from the presidency of Carysfort so that I could go back to Chile. Her predecessor had nominated me for the job in 1974. She and her Council would now have to initiate the process of replacing me. They didn't seem at all keen on the idea. They were still deliberating about it a few months later when the Irish government made an unexpected decision of its own about Carysfort.

On 3 February 1986, the Minister for Education sent a letter to the College and, on the same day, announced publicly in the national parliament that, as part of an urgent fiscal-rationalisation programme, the cabinet had decided to close Carysfort as a teacher-training college. The country's birth rate had been falling, the state had too many teachers, and the government, in an effort to reduce an oversized national debt, had decided that the country could do with one less teacher-training facility.

The merits of the decision to discontinue training teachers in Carysfort were debatable. You could argue the case either way. But the measure itself was imposed with a staggering lack of sensitivity and an apparently total absence of planning, preparation, or foresight about the far-reaching ramifications of the closure. It was announced without consultation – or even the courtesy of a single day's advance notice – to an institution that had served the Irish people with steady and self-sacrificing effort for over a hundred years. As a public measure it aroused the kind of controversy that was inevitable in the wake of a decision that was so hastily reached, so clumsily executed, and so wasteful of public resources in the way it was carried into effect.

I found myself, overnight, in the eye of a storm. But, inadvertently, the closure of Carysfort brought one unexpected benefit to me. It meant that, when the last cohort of teachers graduated from the college in 1988, I could consider my work in Ireland completed. I would be free to retire and return to Chile, with no unfinished business and relatively little cause for backward looks or regrets. This didn't happen immediately. It would take two years – and something that felt like a war of nerves and attrition involving stand-offs with two successive governments and three different ministers for education – before guarantees were eventually secured for the future of the Carysfort staff.

What was to become of the college itself was still the subject of discussions between the government and the Sisters of Mercy who owned Carysfort when I left Ireland early in 1989. There was a proposal – and the Taoiseach and Minister for Education seemed favourable towards it – to turn the beautiful old campus into a National College of Music and Dramatic Arts, with the existing Dublin College of Music as its nucleus. This project aimed to provide a much-needed expansion of facilities for music-education in Ireland, and ample new amenities for programmes in the dramatic arts and courses in modern languages.

As for myself, my work in Carysfort was finished, with only the inevitable tidying up of papers and files to see to, when the last group of teachers graduated from the college in July 1988. I retired two months later, and began to prepare for my return to Chile. By the time I left Dublin for South America again on 20 March, 1989, the files of the president's office were in the archives, and the records of Carysfort as a teacher-training college were beginning to gather dust on one of the shelves of Irish educational history. It was a relief, or at least a distraction from sad and confused feelings, to turn my mind to the details of my return to Chile.

Cochabamba, where I went for a brief language refresher-course in March 1989, was a far bleaker experience the second time around. For one thing I was desperately lonely. This was no sabbatical try-out. I had left my family and friends on the other side of the world, and I was setting out for Chile with painfully-acute feelings about the finality of the step I was taking. A heavy line had been drawn under the life and work that lay behind me. I was coming to South America to stay this time. My hope was somehow, somewhere, to shape a new life. But as yet, the future had no name, no place, not even the comforting contours of a probable destination or a likely future activity, to give it clarity.

My journal reflected the note of bleakness almost as soon as I landed on Bolivian soil:

> From La Paz
> with a destination still to reach,
> my energies flowed forward feelinglessly,
> and the postcard I scribbled was buoyant,
> brittle, only incipiently cautious,
> a last skater's arabesque
> on the ice of a departing spring.
> In Cochabamba
> I sank suddenly into the void
> of another hemisphere's warm unseasonableness
> an empty evening, a silent room.
> a loneliness so desolate
> I don't want to know it
> ever again.

And on that comfortless note I survived until my language-course was over and it was time for me to go down to Chile. My return had none of the happy excitement of my first arrival in the country in 1984. It had even less of the sweet-sad feelings of my departure from Santiago for Dublin in June 1985. The extraordinary buoyancy of spirit I had known during those months of sabbatical leave in Chile was like something from a lost Eden that I could hardly bear to think about; and reading my favourite Jorge Luis Borges sonnet only made the void I was in now feel deeper. My situation was full of loneliness and uncertainty.

I was met at the airport this time by Sisters Breda Colbert and Anne Langan of the Cross and Passion community, and in their little house in Lo Hermida in east Santiago, I spent the first three months after my return. I had no clear plan or immediate work-project of my own yet. I wanted to wait and see, to learn what I could, and eventually to find a way of making some personal contribution to the struggle against poverty, especially for needy children and young people.

But, as the weeks went by, I found myself growing increasingly anxious and uneasy. I went through acute bouts of doubt and self-reproach as I began to realise that I wasn't cut out for work in a poor *población*. Each passing day made it clearer to me that I wasn't going to find any real foothold or convincing sense of personal engagement in the parish activities and development projects of the little Cross and Passion community where I was staying. Worse still, I felt impatient with myself for my long weeks of inactivity. I desperately wanted to find some way of making a contribution to the struggle against the misery that I could see so clearly all around me, but all I could find inside myself was a disabling sense of uncertainty and anxiety. It was winter in Santiago, and a damp chill of self-doubt, like the cold foggy weather outside, seemed to be settling on my heart.

During my stay in Chile in 1984-85 I had never thought of Valparaíso as a place where I might live or work, even temporarily. The opposite, if anything, would have been true. I had gone there only once, to make a retreat in February 1985, and although I looked forward beforehand to visiting the city that had been so romantically eulogised in the little Irish poem I had learned in school long ago, I ended up with strangely reserved feelings after my first visit to the famous old seaport. My short stay there had produced a mixture of strong impressions that I found it hard to make sense of afterwards.

Friends had warned me then that Valparaíso, like San Francisco in California, is a city where earthquakes occur from time to time, so I wasn't altogether taken by surprise when a series of strong tremors began to shake the city soon after the retreat began. The newspapers speculated about the possibility of a full-scale earthquake, and there was a palpable sense of foreboding in the air. This turned out to be well-founded because one week later, just after I left again for Santiago, a frightening earth-movement damaged several regions of central Chile, including Valparaíso. So I learned my first lesson about earthquakes – you can't come to terms with them either before or after they happen. All you can do is try to forget about them unless or until they happen again.

The other impression I had of Valparaíso as a result of that brief visit in 1985 was that it seemed to be a city in steep commercial decline and sad physical decay, a place of wretched and highly-visible poverty. Nowhere else, not even in the poor areas I was familiar with in Santiago, had I seen so much evidence of a bare hand-to-mouth struggle for survival. The worn-out shoes, cast-off clothes, fifth-hand goods, the bits and pieces of salvaged household furniture, the sheer poverty of the trading that went on in its many untidy street-markets was a shock to me. I remember thinking that some of the old boots I saw for sale along Avenida Argentina near the Jesuit Retreat House were so battered they might have done time in a Russian labour camp.

Another thing that struck me during that first visit was that it was unexpectedly difficult to get to the seafront, or go for a walk along the shore, at least from the part of the city where I was staying. You could sense that the ocean was close by there somewhere, but it seemed oddly inaccessible behind a long zone of dockside-warehousing, stacked containers, railway-tracks, giant cranes, and spaghetti swirls of fast-moving traffic. Besides, the naval docks were bristling just then with the steely-grey warships of the Chilean Navy, and these were associated strongly in my mind with the repressive arm of the Pinochet dictatorship which they helped to keep in power.

All in all, I left Valparaíso at the end of February 1985 without much regret. In fact, because of the continuing earth-tremors, I think I left it with a real sense of relief. My time on retreat there had been a strange experience too. It was tinged with a sense of foreboding about an ending of some kind that was imminent in my life. I had a series of disturbing intimations of death that I found hard to deal with. So I was glad, on the whole, to get out of Valparaíso on the afternoon of Friday, 1 March, 1985 and take the bus back to Santiago.

Two days later, most of central Chile, including the city of Valparaíso and the surrounding province, was shattered by a frightening earthquake. Practically everybody had sensed that it was coming, but nobody could do anything about it except wait and pray, and hope that they'd be alive and unharmed and still have a roof over their heads when it was all over.

I was not to see Valparaíso again until more than four years later, in July 1989. By then a great deal had happened in my life. I had known endings but, as yet, no firm new beginning. Carysfort was closed. I had left Ireland. After my language-course in Bolivia, I had spent nine uneasy weeks in Lo Hermida in east Santiago. The brown mud of the Santiago *poblaciónes* during that cold winter seemed to match the damp chill of uncertainly that had been gaining on me ever since I had come back to Chile. So I was glad when Anne Langan invited me to go with her to the old Cross and Passion house in Valparaíso for a weekend during the winter holidays.

Playa Ancha, where this former Passionist school was located, turned out to be a wide, sprawling, densely-populated hill on the southern fringe of the city. It was a part of Valparaíso that I hadn't seen before, and I was delighted to find that there was a small sandy beach and a long rocky shore within easy walking distance of the house. I had been pining for the sea during the months since I left Ireland. Cochabamba and Santiago were both inland cities, and I had begun to feel an acute sense of being landlocked, on top of all my other ills.

But I had practical reasons for wanting to go to Valparaíso that July too. Mary MacGuiness, a Columban friend from San Antonio days, had told me about a Justice and Peace organisation that might welcome the services of a volunteer. When I went to their office in Santiago, they said the Valparaíso branch needed somebody just then. My visit to the coast would give me a chance to find out if there was something I could really do down there. Besides, Anne Langan had told me about a residence for students located in the former Cross and Passion school in Playa Ancha where the community had made its premises available to provide low-budget accommodation for needy university students. The project was in constant need of support and finance, and Anne thought I might be able to help.

We arrived in Valparaíso in the middle of an all-out winter storm, the like of which I hadn't seen since I was a child growing up beside the Atlantic nearly five decades before. That week, a cargo ship was wrecked almost within sight of the coast, with the loss of all her crew. It was a shock to realise that a South Pacific storm could wreak such lethal havoc in an age of advanced communications and sophisticated marine technology. It was my first introduction to a phenomenon that I'd get to know very well afterwards, the fact that the Pacific can turn into a brown destructive monster when it suddenly decides to blow up a certain kind of wild, wintry rainstorm.

But, in some odd way, while that storm frightened me, it also attracted me to the old seaport which I hadn't thought much of before. The Justice and Peace organisation welcomed my offer of help too. They were planning a field programme that I could take part in, a series of in-service courses for teachers, a group badly discriminated against and deeply demoralised during the years of the dictatorship. After my time in Carysfort, I felt that teachers might be one group whose language and concerns I had some hope of understanding.

The university hostel welcomed me as well, and brought me into contact with another familiar constituency, young third-level students. It was there that I met Rebecca Perez Roldan, the Playa Ancha neighbour from whom I was eventually to rent a tiny rooftop apartment overlooking the ocean. Although stone-deaf as a result of near-fatal meningitis in childhood, she ran the student hostel in a caring and efficient way as a voluntary lay-helper of the Cross and Passion community. Her reputation for multiplying the loaves and fishes for needy students and their friends intrigued me.

I stayed in a house near the hostel while I was searching for a place to live, and it was during those early months, at a time when she was busy working out a highly-creative solution to my housing problem, that Rebecca mentioned summer holidays one day. She was planning to visit friends in Punta Arenas in January or February and hoped to see as much as possible of Patagonia on the way. She wondered if I had holiday plans of my own, or if I'd be interested in joining her on this trip to the far south of Chile. The only thing was, this would have to be a journey by sea.

'In a Spanish galleon, following the path of the sun, to the shores of Tierra del Fuego?' I asked her.

'Please write that down,' she said in her practical way, in case she hadn't lip-read correctly. She looked at the bit of paper, shook her head with a puzzled expression, and then spread her arms wide in an eloquent Chilean gesture of incomprehension.

'¿Y por qué no?' she said cheerfully. 'And, why not?'

5

A MERMAID'S PURSE

By the time I began preparing the journey to Patatgonia with Rebecca in January 1990, things were beginning to look hopeful again in my life. My move to South America following the closure of Carysfort, which felt like such a bleak mistake during the long winter months of 1989 in Santiago, had begun to show brighter horizons. I knew now that I could live and work in Valparaiso. I was beginning to see a place for writing in my life. If I were lucky it would help to generate funds for my project of educating poor children.

But there was one problem, an impending decision involving fundamental changes in my life, that was still unresolved. It weighed heavily on my mind as I made preparations for the journey to the far south. This was the question of formally separating from the Mercy community in Dublin where I had been a member for thirty-three years. It would be at least as difficult and definitive a step as leaving Ireland for Chile had been in the first instance.

My commitment to the life and work of the Mercy congregation for more than thirty years between the 1950s and the 1980s was as whole-hearted as I could make it. For me, it had been a good, challenging and engaging life. But by 1989 a great many things had changed, both inside me and around me. After my experience of sabbatical leave in Chile in 1984-5, the closure of Carysfort College was by far the most signifcant event to make an impact on my life. Institutions like Carysfort, which were once vitally necessary for the training of Irish teachers, had begun as works of social beneficence. They were no longer needed in the more prosperous and self-sufficient society that had now begun to emerge in Ireland. But closer to the bone for me was the realisation that the closure of the college presented me with the opportunity and the impetus to make a personal change that had been on my mind for some time. Three decades of work in an active eduacational community had gradually convinced me of my need for a more solitary and less public kind of life.

I had always been secretly attracted to the old Celtic-Christian idea of solitude, reflection, prayer and a life close to nature, but my efforts to be practical about contributing to social justice in some small corner of the world had seemed to point me in almost the opposite direction. As Helder Camara put it, it's hard to keep the soul of a jeep in the body of a Cadillac, and in an age when millions of people had to live wretchedly in overcrowded cities, solitude seemed a luxury that might only burden me with a sense of privilege and unease.

But following my first visit to Chile in 1984, I had begun to dream of finding a way to combine the need for solitude with some kind of concrete contribution to the struggle against poverty, especially through the education of disadvantaged young people. I wanted to find an urban retreat, a quiet spot, but not too far removed from where poor people had to live and struggle. In effect, I wanted to live simply and set aside whatever I could for the education of poor children.

The trouble was that I found it painful even to *think* about leaving the Mercy community in Dublin where I had spent so many good years. In the beginning it seemed an almost unimaginable step for me. I had entered the novitiate at the age of nineteen, and my identity was closely bound up with the experience of living in a community. My family and friends would find it hard to understand why I was moving out now too, since I had no quarrel with the Mercy congregation nor it with me, as far as I knew. On the contrary, I was grateful for the kind of life it had helped me to live, an austere formation when I was young and easy-going, and the challenge of increasingly responsible work assignments in the years that followed. Above all, I valued the tradition of compassion and solidarity with poor people that was the historic *raison d'etre* of the Mercy communities. Putting all that behind me by some formal and inevitably public act of separation wasn't going to be easy. I found myself procrastinating, and I wondered if I'd ever have the courage to take the first step towards formal disaffiliation.

But then something happened that in an odd, reactive way, moved me closer to a decision. Carysfort was put up for sale: convent, college, parklands, woods, meadows, playing fields, the lake, the gardens, the beautiful and historic old buildings, the brand new extensions, the spacious college campus. All of it was packaged, advertised, and – predictably enough – sold within a short time to a syndicate of property developers. Now, I had no strong views, one way or the other, about the sale of the Carysfort lands, although I was personally sad to see them go. I had loved and enjoyed those beautiful grounds and hoped others could go on doing the same. I fancied I knew every tree in the park, by sight if not by name. But as the central asset of an increasingly unsalaried and ageing community with commitments in Africa as well as in Ireland, it had been on the cards for some time that the lands might have to go.

The thing that did trouble me was the selling of the college itself. I just couldn't believe that it was rolled in as one more item in a flat commercial property deal. During my last months in Ireland there were still hopes – uncertain and much-deferred hopes – of getting government approval and finance to turn it into a National College of Music and Dramatic Arts, an amenity for which its spacious period buildings and privileged location seemed to make it particularly appropriate. A working party, set up by the Minister for Education, Mary O'Rourke, at the request of the Taoiseach, Charles Haughey, in spring 1988, had reported favourably on the need, feasibility and approximate costing of this project. The hope that such a development would eventually take place on the campus had been the one bright spot on an otherwise dark horizon during those final, difficult months in Carysfort.

So what had happened since I left Ireland? Why was the college up for sale now on the international property market? I didn't know, and it shocked me at some deep level when it was sold to a consortium of property developers. Had generations of Irish women dedicated their lives and energies, their personal and communal resources, their days and nights of hard work, their frugal and devoted years – so that something like this might happen? So that the college might be stripped down and treated as one more saleable asset? At first I couldn't believe it, and then I couldn't understand it.

The day in 1989 when I heard that Carysfort College had been sold to a consortium of property developers was almost as painful as that strange, snowy morning in February 1986 when the announcement of its closure as a teacher-training college was delivered to us without warning, in a letter from the Minister for Education, in the middle of an ordinary working week. It was a moment of shock, disbelief, anger and uncomprehending sadness. I felt angry with the government, with the community, with Ireland, and more obscurely, with myself. I sat down the same evening and drafted my letter of disaffiliation.

But reactive energy is a doubtful motive force at the best of times, so I never finished the letter. It was a raw script, in any case, full of painful emotion and imprecise argument. I tore it up, and some time later, started a different one. I re-drafted this other letter more than a dozen times and I noticed how, each time I re-wrote it, my focus shifted, as in all truth, it had to, from those broad public issues to the more personal grounds where my option for a different and more solitary kind of life really lay. This letter – and the difficulty of mustering up the courage to tell my family and friends that I was leaving the Mercy community after so many years – was the bit of unfinished business that weighed most heavily on my mind that January, as I made preparations for my journey to Tierra del Fuego. So much so that, during the outward phase of the voyage, I didn't even allow myself to think what the journey might ultimately mean for me. Would it help me to find a hidden continuity with the distant and sustaining world of childhood that lay at an even deeper level than my three decades in the convent? Would it help me to enter into my new life in South America with more understanding and empathy towards people who had been so deeply oppressed by my own people, my fellow Europeans? Would it give me the courage to face more clear-sightedly the next stage of my personal journey, which I could only dimly envisage as some continuation of the struggle against poverty that had brought me into the Sisters of Mercy in the first place?

I had no clear thoughts or questions, much less specific hopes or expectations, as I prepared to go to Tierra del Fuego in January 1990. And yet, in some obscure part of my being, I did sense that this journey was going to make a difference, that it would, at the very least, be a significant marker at the beginning of a new phase in my life. In any event, I had waited so long for it, I was determined to enjoy it.

Rebecca, my travelling companion, had reasons of her own for wanting to make a journey to Patagonia, but the one goal that we both shared was to reach Patagonia by sea. For Rebecca, it was a kind of pilgrimage, I think, in memory of her father, who had spent a lifetime in the Chilean navy. He had sailed these waters from Valparaíso to the Magellan Straits many times, most memorably when he went to Antarctica with President Gonzalez Videla in the 1940s. On that occasion he was part of a national expedition to vindicate Chile's claim to sovereignty over a small wedge of the great white continent and to raise the national flag over a sliver of frozen territory that stretches all the way to the South Pole. This territory would be named for Bernardo O'Higgins, Chile's liberator who dreamed of bringing an Irish colony to the south of Chile. He never managed to carry out that particular project because, like many another South American liberator, he died in exile, pining for the country he had freed from Spanish rule.

As for me, I wanted to go to Patagonia by sea because it seemed the only proper way to fulfil my childhood dream. Some obscure determination to carry out that dream in a fitting way had made me turn down an earlier chance of going to the Magellan Straits because I would have had to make the journey, back then, by plane or bus. The opportunity had come up when I was on sabbatical leave in Chile in 1985, and although I was keen at the time to see as much of South America as possible, the shade of the ten-year-old who wanted to follow the path of the sun and arrive on the shores of Tierra del Fuego in a Spanish galleon was still alive enough to feel it would be selling my dreams short if I were to go there in anything as ordinary as a bus or an aeroplane.

By 1990 I knew a good deal more about Chile and was keener than ever to visit the far south. I wanted to see the wild sea-channels below Chiloe, the uninhabited islands of coastal Patagonia, the volcanoes, glaciers, fjords, steppelands, penguin-habitats, and the sites of old shipwrecks and abandoned forts along the Magellan Straits. I also wanted to visit one of the world's great nature reserves, a vast area of pristine Patagonian territory called Las Torres del Paine, which had been designated by the United Nations as a world biosphere reserve a few years earlier.

But when Rebecca went to look for passages on a ship that would take us from Valparaíso to the Straits in January 1990, she couldn't find any. There was no passenger service operating between Valparaíso and the Magellan Straits anymore. What was worse, we couldn't even get passages on a cargo ship. In the end, we had to give up the idea of setting out by sea from Valparaíso. The only vessels regularly covering the route were navy ships and special cargo-transports, and neither of them would take us on as passengers. A Playa Ancha neighbour, who was an engineer in the Merchant Marine, gave us some good advice: 'Forget about setting out by sea from Valparaíso,' he said. 'What you have to do is travel overland as far as Puerto Montt, and you'll have no trouble finding a ship that will take you the rest of the way from there. It's still close on two thousand kilometres to the Straits.'

If we wanted a luxury trip we could book a passage on one of the special cruisers that made tourist-sailings through the Patagonian sea-channels during the holiday season. But we were on a tighter budget, so the thing to do was to get a passage on one of the cargo boats of the Navimag Shipping Company. Navimag's vessels operated a regular cargo and passenger service between Puerto Montt and Puerto Natales all year round, except when difficult weather conditions made the journey too dangerous. Our friend the engineer worked for Navimag and promised to get us two good berths.

About ten days later he turned up with passages for a cargo vessel called, promisingly enough, the *Tierra del Fuego*. Although the name didn't mean she was going all the way to the island of that name, she'd land us within striking distance of it. In any case, we'd eventually have to cross the Magellan Straits by ferry. Rebecca was pleased to hear that we'd be landing in Puerto Natales. She had an old Valparaíso friend living there, and it was only a short distance from Las Torres del Paine.

The *Tierra del Fuego*, our engineer friend told us, was a solid cargo ship, built in Europe and registered in the port of Valparaíso. Her regular beat was this southern route through the labyrinth of uninhabited islands and sea-channels that stretch between Puerto Montt and Puerto Natales. Most of these islands and channels, a typical wild landscape of the far south of Chile, are located in Patagonia, the elusive region I had searched for, in vain, long ago in my sister's school atlas.

January is high summer in Chile and the best time to go travelling in the rainy south of the country, but the month was nearly over by the time Rebecca and I were able to set out on our journey to the Magellan Straits. We had packed rainwear, warm clothes, stout shoes, and even extra-strong umbrellas, all on the advice of acquaintances who had been in that part of the world before us, some of them for long periods during naval service. It seemed an odd way to prepare for a summer holiday but we were advised to take no chances.

The first leg of the journey was a pleasant two-hour bus ride from Valparaíso to Santiago through the hills of the coastal Cordillera north of the capital. We passed through the neat vineyards of Casablanca, and skirted the irrigated fertile valleys that lie in the folds of the mountains just north of Santiago. After that there was a run of ochre-and-grey hills so continuous that the government, years ago, cut two long tunnels under the mountains to shorten what would otherwise be a very roundabout hilly route from the coast to the capital.

We arrived in Santiago just before six o'clock on a hot summer's evening. We had an hour to wait for the train to Puerto Montt. I sat on a bench surrounded by our bulky-looking luggage and made my first entry in the notebook I had bought to keep a log of the journey:

> Sitting in Estacion Central, Santiago's main train-station, a busy place, a full-blown commercial and open-marketing area with throngs of people in continuous movement all around. Here you can shop, eat, wander about and buy pretty much anything you need or fancy or can afford. The range runs from the cheapest imported goods to assorted Chilean souvenirs and craftwork. This is obviously an older and poorer part of the city. Nearly half the people of Chile live now in the big urban sprawl of Santiago, and the overcrowding shows – in the packed trains of the Metro, in the thronged sidewalks of busy central-city areas like this one, but most of all in the spreading *poblaciónes pobres* that ring the outskirts of the city.
>
> It's uncomfortably hot here in the centre of the city today. Santiago is an inland capital located in a sheltered valley of the Andes and, because of that, condemned to the discomforts of becoming an increasingly unhealthy smog-trap, especially in late autumn and winter. It's an attractive city, though. Odd unexpected one-off hills show up suddenly near the centre, and away in the distance, ranges, folds and peaks of the blue-grey Cordillera form a high snow-dusted circle along the horizon. It's a picturesque place when the smog clears and allows you to see it properly.
>
> Santiago is probably one of the most genuinely-cultured cities in South America, and a very good place to visit. But as for living in it? Well, give me the up-and-down hilly slopes and salty airs of Valparaíso any time, especially on a sweltering mid-summer's day like this. On the coast today it was cool and breezy. Here in the capital

it's like a damped-down furnace.

Valparaíso with its forty hills, crumbling mansions, untidy streetmarkets, uneven earthquaked streets – and even its sad poverty – holds me in a way that this busy, crowded capital never did. There's nowhere else in Chile, or in the world maybe, quite like the great half-moon bay of Valparaíso with its forty-odd hills. (Getting nostalgic for the old port already – and only two-and-a-half hours out?)

This will be my first train journey in Chile, not counting city-runs on the French-designed Santiago Metro. Our overnight journey to Puerto Montt promises to be a long one.

To call it a long journey was probably the kindest thing I could say about it afterwards. For nearly fifteen hours our ancient train, optimistically called a night-express, shook, rattled and rolled, humped, bumped, jolted and swayed noisily down the one-thousand-and-sixteen kilometres of uneven track that carried us from Santiago to the small southern seaport of Puerto Montt. It had taken me about the same length of time but a lot less wear-and-tear, to get from Europe to South America nine months earlier. That was an air-journey, though. This was definitely something else.

I had to forget about *The Irish Times* I had kept for reading in the train when darkness fell and there was no more scenery to be viewed. During most of the long night I couldn't read, I couldn't write, I couldn't sleep. I couldn't even make myself comfortable. All I could do was look out the window at the little groups of people who huddle at train-stations in the middle of the night. I watched the dark countryside rolling past, saw the stars dodging in and out between the high peaks of the Cordillera, and listened to Rebecca and another passenger snoring comfortably on either side of me.

I came to the conclusion that Chilean Railways mustn't have invested in new rolling stock for this line since 1937, the year I was born. In fact I felt young and spry by comparison with some of the ancient carriages that made up this rattling old train. I distracted myself for a while, juggling with the lines of a negro spiritual to put together the ultimatum I meant to convey to Rebecca about our future land travels in Chile, when she woke up in the morning:

> God gave Noah the rainbow sign.
> No more railways, the road next time.

When dawn broke over the Andes – a beautiful sight even to my glazed and sleepless eyes – we had left the dusty ochre-and-grey hills of the coastal Cordillera and central Chile far behind us. We had passed through the rich fruit-producing regions to the south of the capital, and now we were travelling through a cooler, greener, and altogether more pastoral and rainy-looking countryside. It reminded me of Ireland.

Rebecca woke up, stretched herself like a well-rested cat, and leaned over to look out the window at the pleasant green countryside rolling past the window. With the sense of well-being you can only give voice to at seven-thirty in the morning if you've had a good night's sleep, she opened her eyes wide and said, *Mira! Qué hermosa!* And a lovely sight it surely was. Even I had to nod in wry agreement.

It was a rich landscape, full of broad sloping pastures and well-timbered land where streams and rivers flowed into deep wooded valleys. Lush green meadows were set, emerald-like, against the backdrop of the towering blue-and-white snow-capped heights of the Cordillera. A gentle early-morning mist, a sort of mild rising haze, made it even more sun-shadowed and peaceful-looking. You could only admire and be grateful for such scenery. Besides, neither Rebecca nor the landscape was responsible for the discomforts of the long wakeful train journey that had brought us into this beautiful south-Chilean dawn. But that didn't prevent me from having a suppressed impulse to put the blame on *somebody*.

Nearly four hours later we arrived in Puerto Montt. After the train had clattered into the old railway station and we gathered our luggage together on the platform I saw a notice in large black letters on one of the walls: *You have now arrived in the most southerly railway-station in the world.* In the circumstances I felt that was a cause for rejoicing.

We had covered the first 1136 kilometres of our journey from Valparaíso. For the next part of the trip, the almost two thousand kilometres which, our guide-book assured us, stretched between Puerto Montt and Puerto Natales along the Patagonian sea-channels, we would be passengers on the good ship, *Tierra del Fuego*.

The breath of small islands, or maybe just certain sights and sounds that brought back memories of the weather-beaten islanders my mother used to welcome to our house when I was small, struck me vividly the evening Rebecca and I arrived in Puerto Montt and went down to the harbour at Angelmó to see where our ship would sail from the following day. The *Tierra del Fuego* was drawn up at the Navimag berth having her engines checked and part of her cargo loaded in preparation for the next day's journey. We discovered we'd have nearly twenty-four hours to rest and see the city before embarking for Puerto Natales the following afternoon.

My first priority was to get some sleep. I badly needed a few hours of rest in a comfortable bed to smooth the vibrations of our long rattling train journey from Santiago out of my jangled nervous system. But by one of those small misfortunes that sometimes befall budget travellers, it turned out that the house where we were staying was only a block away from the railway line which ran parallel to the seaward edge of the city. So I had barely sunk into my first soothing slumber when I was jolted awake again by the familiar clang of a moving train. It was setting up a series of small earth tremors that seemed to reach right in under my bed. Could it be the same old bone-shaker that had brought us to Puerto Montt last night, setting off in the direction of the capital again? It sounded – it even felt – like it. God help those poor passengers, I thought, as the noise receded and I drifted off to sleep for a second time, and God grant there'll be no more trains using the most southerly railway station in the world until I have a chance to get a few decent hours of rest.

This time we were lucky. There was relatively little movement of trains in or out of Puerto Montt that day. Most people, we discovered afterwards, were wiser than us, or more experienced about making the long journey from Santiago to the south. They travelled in the comfortably-sprung, long-distance sleeper buses that had been taking business from the trains for several years past, which, no doubt, contributed to the closure of Puerto Montt railway station not long afterwards. The last time I saw it the city was considering turning part of it into a heritage centre.

After a few hours rest we felt refreshed enough to set out on our first round of sightseeing in the south. Puerto Montt seemed to be an oddly scattered place, a small straggling up-and-down hilly city that had probably sprung up originally around the tiny harbour of Angelmó and gradually spread out from there. Apart from one long, open, well-defined boundary on the seaward side that looked out across the Gulf of Reloncaví, it would be hard to say where the city began or ended. The small harbour and open seafront were easily its most attractive features, especially the long promenade with landscaped green spaces that skirted the city and the gulf for more than two kilometres, and gave sweeping views of hills and headlands, low distant islands, high grey-blue mountains, and even a snow-capped volcano on the landward side. The city looked directly out over the peaceful, navigable, semi-enclosed waters of the Gulf of Reloncaví.

A brisk walk in the sea-air along this pleasant waterfront brought us down to the small harbour at Angelmó. Here everything was bustling with activity. The place was full of people, traffic, noise, and a sort of constant, crowded, jostling movement. The little quaysides were thronged with buyers and sellers who moved around between street-markets, craft-stalls, shops and small fish-restaurants. These, in their turn, were busy with the endless comings and goings of islanders, market-people, travellers, tourists, and local housewives buying fresh sea-produce and vegetables. Islanders from Chiloe were unloading crates and baskets from small boats. Launches and little rowboats were ferrying people across to Isla Tenglo on the opposite side of the channel. Angelmó is situated well out on the fringes of Puerto Montt, but there was no doubt at all that this was the real, traditional heart of the city.

After we checked our embarkation time at the Navimag office, we went for a leisurely stroll around the harbour area. It was crammed almost to bursting point that day. There was a constant movement of boats in an out of the harbour but most of them were very small craft. The *Tierra del Fuego* was by far the biggest vessel in sight. She was scheduled to leave for Puerto Natales the following day, but she couldn't set sail until about three o'clock in the afternoon because the harbour-waters were too shallow, and a ship of her size could only sail when the tide was full.

Puerto Montt is a city of relatively recent origin, founded by government charter a few decades after Chile got its independence from Spain in the nineteenth century. But the old harbour district at Angelmó had been a regular centre of commerce between the islands of the Chiloe archipelago and the Chilean mainland, from time immemorial. The settlement around the harbour gradually developed into a modest seaport, and this, in time, grew into a thriving commercial and industrial centre, especially when the Chilean government invited farming colonists from Germany to develop the lands to the north of the city towards the end of the nineteenth century.

Something about the air and landscape of Puerto Montt felt familiar to me almost from the first moment I stepped out into the street of this small coastal town with the damp, windy, unpredictable airs of a place that has to do its business against a backdrop of highly changeable sea-weathers. As a west-of-Ireland woman I should have felt at home in such a place. But the creeping comforts of the mild climate around Valparaíso had been growing on me over the last few months. In central Chile, cold, wet weather generally confines itself to a few well-defined months of winter. You know, as a rule, when to take out warm clothes and have rainwear at the ready. Puerto Montt, on the other hand, was the kind of place where it rained any day of the year it felt like it. Even in summer the weather could suddenly turn wet and windy within half an hour. Very like Ireland.

But we were lucky on our first evening there. It was fine and sunny when we set out for our walk. The view from the seafront was clear and peaceful, full of the tones and shades that follow recent showers. Shifting cloud-formations moved shadowy patches across the calm sunny surface of the gulf. Low islands and high snow-capped mountains formed a broken ring along the distant horizon. Irish landscapes are celebrated for their varied shades of green, but Puerto Montt seemed to me that evening to have an even more striking spectrum of blues. On a calm, sunlit evening the Gulf of

Reloncaví is a memorably lovely stretch of enclosed silvery-blue waters.

The German colonists who came to settle near Puerto Montt at the invitation of the Chilean government towards the end of the nineteenth century gradually transformed the countryside to the north of the city into a pleasant, well-cultivated pastoral landscape that has no real parallel in any other part of Chile. The colonists, mostly farming people from rural Catholic areas in southern Germany, cleared the forests, built wooden houses with steep tiled roofs, and set about farming the land with practical German industry and efficiency. They maintained links with Europe, imported machinery and breeding stock, and were soon producing meat, dairy goods, timber and a range of farm products of exceptionally high quality. Their pork and dairy produce in particular – and a little item which was to become characteristic of the area, a range of delicious German *kuchenes* or fruit pies – would soon become famous throughout Chile.

The native tribes who lived to the north of Puerto Montt, the indigenous inhabitants of the rainy and heavily-forested lands that were home to the warlike Araucanian Indians, were people with a very different rhythm of life. They had an almost totally distinct conception of their relationship to the earth from the newly-arrived Europeans. As a result, the colonisation process brought tensions and troubles that weren't easily resolved. There are still problems over tribal lands in parts of southern Chile almost a century later, though not so much nowadays in the areas originally settled by the German colonists.

One of the small ironies of Chilean history in its immediate post-independence era is the story of how the hitherto-unsubdued tribes of the Araucanian south were brought under the rule of central government. Rebecca likes to claim ancestral links with the Araucanian Indians on her maternal grandfather's side. She takes pride in the connection because these particular tribes fought stubbornly against the Spaniards for centuries. They would boast that, after more than three hundred years of repeated military incursions, the Spanish king's writ never really ran in their territories.

The irony lay in how quickly they were subdued, during the course of the nineteenth century, by their own fellow countrymen. Their integration into the new state was the work of a series of independent Chilean governments who built railways and police-barracks, deployed military garrisons, brought in European settlers, encouraged forest clearance, and eventually brought the tribes into a certain wary alignment with the new national state. But it has always remained a slightly uneasy and less-than-satisfactory relationship, especially from the point of view of the tribespeople. The old fires of revolt are liable to kindle again, from time to time, in true Araucanian hearts.

The German colonists, for their part, systematically cleared and transformed their own region of the country, and succeeded in giving the landscape a cultivated, South German look which eventually opened the way for one of Chile's most thriving regional tourist industries. The countryside north of Puerto Montt is a picturesque place of lakes and woods, mountains and volcanoes, rivers, waterfalls and rolling green pastures. This verdant landscape, one of the most pleasing and beautiful in all Chile, attracts a steady stream of national and overseas visitors. Its appeal to foreign tourists is heightened by its proximity to the great nature reserves and forested Andean frontier passes that link Chile with Argentina.

There was a slow fiery sunset over the Gulf of Reloncavi when Rebecca and I finished our sightseeing in Puerto Montt that evening. We lingered for a while along the waterfront to enjoy the unexpected, almost dramatic, beauty of it. Flares of luminous peach-and-gold light flared out from behind a broken rack of low, dark clouds. Further away, where the sea merged with the deeper blue of the islands along the rim of the gulf, the clouds opened for a space and we could see layers and folds of mountains, range after range of grey-blue ridges receding into the distance. Behind them were the faint, jagged, snow-capped peaks of the Andes, but these were so far away, they looked subdued and almost insubstantial from the sunlit seafront where we were standing.

Nearer the city, some distance away to the north, were Puerto Montt's two neighbouring volcanoes. One is a perfectly-shaped, snow-dusted sugar-loaf like an illustration from an old Christmas cookery book. The other is a smallish, irregularly-shaped protuberance peering out close to the flank of the bigger one. The larger of the two, Volcan Osorno, had little wisps of cloud coming and going around its snowy cone that evening. At times its vivid blue-and-white, sugar-loaf perfection changed into something vapourous and rain-menaced. By nightfall it was a chilly grey, wrapped in a damp veil of enveloping mist.

We decided to have our evening meal in one of the small seafood restaurants down by the harbour. This was in the heart of the busy quayside area, a part of the city with a strong flavour of an older life based on boats, fishing, islands, markets, fireside crafts and small farming. When the people of the Chiloe islands come to Puerto Montt to do their buying and selling and exchange their farming and fishing produce for the goods of a more industrialised world, they tend to congregate in this part of the city around Angelmó. Here they eat and drink, meet old friends, and take time to entertain each other and be entertained in some of their own more leisurely and traditional ways. This leaves a perceptible breath of island life and a sense of welcome and hospitality around this part of Puerto Montt that catches the interest and imagination of visitors.

For me it evoked something that was immediately familiar from my childhood. I found myself trying to pin it down that night in my notebook:

> I know these people from the islands.
> I've known them since I was a child.
> Darker-skinned, more weather-beaten than us,
> smelling of the sea and fish and hardship,
> adept at barter and bargaining,
> skillful at fireside crafts, hospitable,
> lovers of music, dancing, drinking, and story-telling.
> Will their way of life be lost in the south of Chile too?
> And what is it about mass-culture that's so seductive?
> The fatal allure of comfort, the slow burn of decay?

It was seven o' clock and there was a pleasant sea-edge to our appetites by the time we sat down to eat. The restaurant window looked directly down over the edge of the water, and the harbour seemed to be almost as busy as when we had first arrived several hours earlier. Small boats were still coming and going. Sacks, crates and loads of fish and vegetables were being carried around on backs and shoulders. Some of the little open-air craft markets were still open for business along the quayside. People were buying and selling and making bargains, or just pushing their way around through the harbour's small spaces.

In the streets around the craft stalls there were scores of visitors wandering about, comparing prices, seeming to get in the way of the more urgent activities of the harbour, and yet being the object of the vendors' most hospitable attentions and exertions. You could tell that some of them were nostalgic returnees, descendants of former Chiloe islanders who lived and worked now in the more urbanised parts of Chile. There were recently-returned political exiles among them too, families back on holidays from countries like Sweden, Germany and Canada, where Chileans found refuge during the years of the Pinochet dictatorship.

'*Un curanto? Un curanto chilote, el plato tipico del sur de Chile…* You can't go away without tasting our *curanto*. You can't even say you've been in Puerto Montt if you haven't eaten a *curanto*.' The proprietors of the little restaurants and *marisquerias* or seafood eateries were lively and insistent. Their sales pitch reminded me of the brochure for a Hollywood cemetery that said, 'You haven't lived if you're not buried here.'

A *curanto* is a tempting dish, if you're not a valetudinarian or a vegetarian. The elements that make up the traditional *curanto*, one of the most typical and tasty dishes of the Chilean south, have a single potent feature in common: they were never meant for delicate stomachs or picky eaters. This is tasty, nourishing, filling, warming and energising food for farming and fishing people who work out of doors in damp, cold weathers. The components of a *curanto* usually include a couple of varieties of fish, as well as meat, sausage, vegetables, two different kinds of potato dumplings, and a highly-appetising range of the region's succulent shellfish.

The traditional *curanto* was cooked out of doors. A hole was dug in the ground and lined with hot stones for the cooking of the meat. More hot stones and coals were heaped on top. Leaves were used to separate one element in the cooking pit from the others. The process seems to have been based on much the same needs and cooking principles as the *fulacht fianniochta* in ancient Ireland, a sort of communal out-of-doors catering system for bands of hunters like the Fianna, or groups of pilgrims on their way to Croagh Patrick or some other holy place. The *curanto* of southern Chile is usually served in generous quantities and is a dish fit to lay an incautious tourist out for anything up to twenty-four hours if he or she is intrepid enough to try the whole range on offer.

But Rebecca had her eye on a different speciality of the Chilean south for our evening meal.

'The wild salmon in this part of the country is a dish fit for a king,' she told me on our way down to the harbour. 'The best salmon in the whole world,' she added modestly.

'How can you be so sure when you haven't tasted a poached salmon from the Bunowen river yet?' I asked her. 'Now, that's God's – and my late father's – own salmon,' I assured her, equally modestly.

Rebecca, like a great many Chileans, is a dedicated connoisseur of seafoods. The country is celebrated for its large and attractive range of shellfish, an impressive array of crusted, crabbed, barnacled, tailed, tentacled, armoured, antennaed species, known collectively as *mariscos*. With its long coastline and rich fishing grounds running from semi-tropical to sub-antarctic waters – not to mention its innumerable fresh-water lakes and rivers – Chile is quite properly famous for the quality and abundance of its seafoods.

So Rebecca was in her element in Angelmó. Her only problem was that we would be spending less than twenty-four hours in the place, not nearly enough time to sample a decent fraction of the tempting range of fish and *mariscos* on offer. The baked salmon, with a special light marisco sauce, was all that she had promised it would be and more besides. Even a Bunowen salmon could hardly have tasted better.

It would probably have done us good to walk home in the brisk night air along the seafront, but we were tired after our travelling and sightseeing so we took a *colectivo*. A *colectivo* is a shared taxi with a fixed route and a standard low fare, one of the great conveniences of Chilean public transport, as far as I'm concerned. *Colectivos* can be found nearly everywhere in the country, even in the smallest towns and villages.

After a while the driver asked me a question I was getting used to.

'*Usted is Alemana?* he inquired politely.

'No,' I said. 'Not German. I'm Irish. *De la Republica de Irlanda.*'

'*Una Irlandesa, pues!* Well then, maybe you can tell me something I've always wanted to know. Is it true that you can see leprechauns' – the word he used was *duendes* – 'in Ireland? I mean do people really see them?'

'If you drink enough strong Irish whiskey,' I assured him, 'you might see any number of leprechauns. A bit like your neighbours here in Chiloe, I'm told that when some of the islanders have the right amount of *chicha* taken, they see the *pincoya. ¿Verdad?*'

He smiled and shook his head wryly. The *chicha* of Chiloe is a fermented apple drink. It can pack an unexpected punch if you take it in sufficiently large quantities. In the warmer parts of Chile, *chicha* is usually made from grapes rather than from apples, but either way it has traditionally been the favourite homemade tipple of the country people.

The *pincoya* is a figure of folk-legend among the islanders of the Chilean south. A benign and beautiful marine creature, it wouldn't be fair really to compare her with an Irish leprechaun. You certainly won't find her mending shoes or guarding pots of gold at the end of a rainbow. Instead, this graceful female figure will sometimes emerge from the sea on a fine evening. Dressed in shimmering algae of tantalising transparency, she'll dance along the edge of the water leaving behind her – when she's in the right mood - a scattering of the fish or shellfish most coveted by the fishermen and housewives of the island.

A reported sighting of the *pincoya* is a good omen for the islanders, especially those who have to make their living the hardest way of all, by diving into the cold southern waters to extract shellfish from the reefs and channels between the islands. It's a type of hardship that calls for the comfort of large warming drafts of *chicha*, or short concentrated ones of *pisco*, a finely-distilled grape liquor, which, however, is more expensive, to get the blood flowing warmly through your veins again once you get back to land.

The mermaids of sea-lore in the northern hemisphere are probably distant cousins of the Chilean *pincoya*. When I was little I loved to read about those strange, singing creatures of the sea who sat on rocks by the shore combing their long, tangled tresses with combs of carved fishbone. But in my heart of hearts I never really *believed* in them. I never expected to find a mermaid perched on a rock when I went down to the sea at Bunowen. And I certainly never shaded my eyes against the sun to look out across Clew Bay in the hope of seeing a mermaid emerge from the water, as I often did in search of a sail or a shape that might turn out to be a schooner or a Spanish galleon.

In Bunowen, near the mouth of the river, I'd sometimes see a young seal that had become separated from its elders and found itself marooned on the rocks after the tide went out, and although I was timid about going close even to those little ones, I still liked watching the big seals whenever they appeared out beyond the rivermouth, dipping and bobbing around in the water on fine evenings. I liked reading about seals, too. Along the west coast of Ireland, seal stories were often close to the folklore about mermaids.

But even though I didn't believe in the existence of mermaids, there was one little item of shore-drift associated with them, at least by name, that I sometimes searched for among the wrack left behind along the high-water mark when the tide went out. This was an odd little pouch, a sort of soft rectangular sheath with spiky corners that we called a mermaid's purse. It was soft and pliable, a bit like a hollow purse made of seaweed, when it came out of the water first, but it dried out quickly and turned hard and brittle when it was away from the brine. This distinctive little piece of sea-drift gradually became associated in my mind with my dream of going to Tierra del Fuego.

The association began on another of those fine evenings when I was sent to the well for water and went down to the beach on my own. I walked along the shore to a favourite bathing spot we called the Kitchen Rocks. I wasn't looking for shells this time. I just wanted to find a mermaid's purse, and I was lucky. I found one that was freshly out of the water, a soft yellowish-brown pouch, not much bigger than my hand. The outgoing tide had left it behind just before I arrived.

I sat down to examine my find and fingered its soft shining texture, knowing that if I put it in my pocket it would soon get dry and brittle and lose all the pliant suppleness of wherever it had come from. But I had to hurry home with water for the tea that evening, so after a while I put the little pouch in my pocket and set off for the house. When I got home I took it out again to have another look, but already, in the few minutes since I left the shore, it had dried out in the heat of my pocket and changed to a darker colour. It had lost all its lovely shiny sea-texture.

That moment – partly of disappointment, and partly of longing for the sea and its mysterious things and places – was charged with feelings that made it linger in my mind for years. I found myself, long afterwards, trying to recapture its flavour:

> My little mermaid's purse,
> smooth, strangely-shaped,
> curled, spike-tipped,
> each protruding point sharp, black,
> from soft and glistening water-brightened sheen,

had stiffened, turned lustreless, then cracked.
Beside the stream, under the well-field wall
I fingered it to soft rhythmatic sounds,
Ti-erra del Fu-ego, where they said
old ships were wrecked near wild Cape Horn.
I'd found no great-sailed galleons, tall brigs or sloops
adrift upon the waters of our bay,
but summer grasses opened like a book
on ice-cold countries, southward, far away.

Some memory of that evening when I found the mermaid's purse came back to me as Rebecca and I stood for a few minutes on the peaceful seafront in Puerto Montt looking out over the rippling night-waters of the Gulf of Reloncaví. Tomorrow we'd be setting sail for those ice-cold countries that I had tried to conjure up long ago in the words of a little verse.

6

INTO PATAGONIA

At Angelmó the next afternoon we found ourselves delayed for an hour, sitting in a wide embarkation area among an assortment of multi-lingual, multi-ethnic, multi-coloured, and multi-aged fellow-passengers some of whom were encumbered with even larger and bulkier amounts of luggage than we were. The delay turned into an extended breathing space that gave us a chance to look around and get acquainted with some of the other travellers. Meanwhile the baggage was being put on board and the last of the big articulated trucks were being waved into their berths at the rear of the ship's long vehicle-hold.

On closer inspection, the *Tierra del Fuego* turned out to be a serviceable, roll-on, roll-off cargo ship with a high quarter-deck and a solid metal hull painted bright red and white. She had green spray-spotted decks, a long ramp, and a deep vehicle bay for trucks, freight containers, and an assortment of smaller vehicles and cargo. She and a companion-ship had the job of maintaining Navimag's regular passenger and general-supply service between Puerto Montt and Puerto Natales all year round, making deliveries at one or two very out-of-the-way places in Chilean Patagonia along the route.

The round trip from Puerto Montt to Puerto Natales usually took about seven or eight days, except when rough weather conditions slowed things down. Fruit, vegetables, wines and processed foods as well as industrial and household goods were shipped south. Sheep, cattle, meat, fish, and especially certain coveted varieties of Patagonian shellfish, such as the succulent scarlet crab known as the *centolla*, were shipped north. Passengers like ourselves could travel in variable comfort either way.

In the waiting area I found myself sitting beside a spry elderly Englishman who was keen to talk. He told me that his grandfather had made what he described as 'a rather comfortable little fortune' in the nitrate mines in northern Chile at the turn of the century. He himself had been travelling in that part of the country for the past three weeks, and he was boarding the *Tierra del Fuego* now because his aim was to get as far as Cape Horn before flying back to Santiago and then home to Manchester.

'Three weeks in the Atacama desert at the height of summer? That must have made a change from winter in the north of England?' I asked him.

'A welcome change,' he said with emphasis.

'You didn't find it too hot, then?'

'Well, just a little at the beginning. But I suffer from arthritis, you know, and I realise now why my grandfather talked such a lot about northern Chile in his old age. When he was in his eighties he wanted to come back again to live here.' He smiled and shook his head thoughtfully.

Starting at Arica near the Peruvian border in the first week of January, the Englishman had made his way south, keeping to the coastal towns and avoiding the dead heat of the interior as far as he could. He had stopped briefly in the cities of Iquique, Tocopilla, Antofagasta and Chañaral, old seaports that had been used for exporting nitrate during the decades of the Chilean mining boom.

'Where was the nitrate exported to?' I asked him.

'The bulk of it to England, Germany, the United States and Mexico,' he said, 'but basically to any country in the world where there was a market – which often meant a war, in progress or impending. Nitrate was used as an explosive in a big way, back then. Much more so than as a fertiliser, in fact.'

On his way from Arica to Santiago he had made a few trips into the interior to see the old settlements where his grandfather had had mining interests, but those visits were disappointing. I asked him if he had been to Vallenar, the northern Chilean city that's named after a west-of-Ireland barony.

'I passed through it,' he said. 'But I didn't know there was any Irish connection. What was the origin of that?'

I told him what I knew, which was sketchy. How Ambrose O'Higgins – father of the famous Bernardo O'Higgins, Chile's liberator – was born in a village in County Sligo early in the eighteenth century. He claimed to be descended from an ancient Irish family with an ancestor named Seán Dubh Ó hUigín who was lord of an area called Ballenary. It would be hard to say for certain now where O'Higgins' ancestral Ballenary was or is. But when he needed a pedigree of nobility to make his way into the upper echelons of Spanish colonial society in eighteenth-century Lima, Baron de Ballenary was the title he chose. He needed to present some patent of nobility in order to advance in Spain's rank-conscious colonial service in South America. He was able and ambitious, and he meant to get to the top.

To be fair to him, Ambrose O'Higgins made his way up on his own merits – his outstanding organisational and administrative ability and his incredible capacity for hard work – rather than on the strength of his supposed ancestral title. He was one of the most effective colonial administrators ever to hold the position of Governor of Chile. During his period of office, new towns were founded, frontier passes through the Andes were opened up, and fortresses, roads, customs posts, mail services and commercial facilities were developed.

'That, of course, was before the country got its independence from Spain,' the Englishman said.

'Yes, in the second half of eighteenth century. Between the 1860s and the 1880s or thereabouts.'

Ambrose O'Higgins had come as a young Irish exile to South America from the port of Cadiz in Spain. Once he settled in the New World, he had risen step-by-step from the lowly rank of a merchant in Lima to that of a successful colonial administrator in the service of the Spanish Crown. He ended up by becoming, not just Governor of Chile, but Viceroy of Peru, an exalted rank for a village boy from County Sligo. Along the way he made bitter enemies of certain Spanish hidalgos who aspired to the rank of Viceroy themselves and took a disdainful view of outsiders like O'Higgins, however able they might be. These enemies eventually succeeded in having O'Higgins deposed from the Viceroyship. Years before that, though, he had seduced a young Chilean girl of good family, and fathered the future Liberator of Chile, Bernardo Riquelme.

'The interesting small-print of history,' the Englishman commented.

For decades Ambrose O'Higgins didn't acknowledge Bernardo Riquelme as his son, and, of course, he never married the boy's mother. His overwhelming ambition got in the way of that. Rising colonial officials were forbidden to marry 'native' women, even if they were daughters of good Creole families, and the elder O'Higgins was the very incarnation of ambition. Still, he did assume responsibility for the education of his son, and had him sent to Spain and England when he realised that the boy had ability. Quite late in his life he also acknowledged him legally so that he could inherit the O'Higgins name and Don Ambrosio's rich estates in Peru. But the boy met his father only once, a brief incognito encounter that took place when he was ten or twelve years old.

'Experiences to steel the will of a future liberator,' the Englishman commented. 'I hadn't realised that Bernardo O'Higgins' father was actually the Spanish King's Viceroy in Peru. So he bred the young revolutionary and republican who was to bring down the empire he had spent his life working for? An interesting story – including how old Ballenary turned into modern Vallenar.'

In the course of our conversation, the Englishman mentioned that he had travelled from Santiago to Puerto Montt by train, and we exchanged commiserations on the experience. Chilean railways had deteriorated almost beyond belief since his grandfather's time, he said, at least if he were to judge by what he had read in the old man's papers. At the beginning of the century the railways had been the back-bone of the mining industry and indispensable to its efficient functioning. Besides, they had provided an excellent passenger service for travellers of three different classes, he assured me.

The nitrate business needed two kind of trains, he explained, railway trains and mule trains. His grandfather had shares in Chilean railways, but he also, at one time, owned more than a hundred mules and employed scores of mule-drivers. These were needed to haul the nitrate from the mines to the railheads. He had been disappointed to discover that the railway line from Santiago to Antofagasta, in which his grandfather once had shares, had completely disappeared. But maybe that was just as well, he reflected wryly, if they weren't going to maintain it properly.

'All in all, it was a worthwhile journey from Arica to Puerto Montt. But quite fatiguing,' he admitted.

'Did you see the places where the ancestral fortune was actually made?' I asked him.

'Not really,' he said after a pause. It had been the greatest disappointment of his trip to find that there was virtually nothing left of the old mining towns and settlements where his grandfather had worked as a young man. One or two uninhabited ghost-towns like Humberstone and Santa Laura, with abandoned machinery rusting away in the sand, silted-up dunes where there had once been streets, houses, stores, and even churches and theatres, were all that remained. The desert was implacable. The nitrate mines had boomed, only to fade equally rapidly, in the decades before and after the First World War. Nitrate was still a highly-priced explosive then. A synthetic substitute for it wouldn't become commercially available until the eve of the Second World War.

I wondered, but didn't like to ask him, if any of his relatives had been killed in the First World War. Had they died in the trenches where so many of the shells that made nitrate-mining in Chile such a profitable business, had finally exploded? Instead, I asked him if his grandfather had known the so-called Nitrate King of Chile, the famous John Thomas North.

This celebrated English mining magnate is still remembered in Chile as an example of the penniless *gringo* who arrived in the country during the nitrate boom, made a fortune in the mines and on the Valparaíso stock-exchange, and then departed, taking his newly-amassed wealth back to England with him. The young man who eventually became Lord North disembarked from a British steam-packet in Valparaíso with, so the story goes, a single five-pound note in his pocket. He left Chile a few decades later with enough money to secure his place among the wealthiest of the English nobility and public recognition for his contribution to the British economy – the Imperial war economy, presumably.

'Yes, my grandfather knew Lord North, of course,' the Englishman said. 'But there was no business connection between them, as far as I know, though they were both here around the time of the Nitrate Wars when Chile fought the Bolivia-Peru alliance. They were dangerous times,' he added.

'A complicated business, that war,' I agreed.

I had read a certain amount about the paradoxically-named Pacific War over nitrate rights, when Chile, covertly backed by wealthy British mining interests, had taken on the combined forces of Bolivia and Peru, and defeated them on land and sea. In the subsequent peace settlement, Chile held on to a large stretch of nitrate-rich desert that she had annexed by force during the conflict. This left Bolivia without access to the sea, a grievance that still rankles deeply in dealings between La Paz and Santiago a full century later.

Why Chile needs that stretch of desert today is a mystery to many people. She certainly doesn't need the extra bit of coast. She already has one of the longest coastlines on the continent. And she hardly needs the development headaches that this far northern desert area is constantly producing for her, either. Flying south from Bolivia to Santiago, I had seen some of those once-valuable, arid, whitish-brown salt and nitrate deposits in the Atacama desert, and it seemed to me that the spread of sand and rock on this part of the globe was truly enormous.

I remember thinking as I looked down from the aeroplane as we flew, hour after hour, over those endless grey-brown landscapes, that if a space-probe from some other planet were to land on this particular part of the earth, the extra-terrestrial explorers might be forgiven for writing us off as an endless, desert-dry wilderness. The areas covered by mountain, rock and sand on this part of the globe have to be seen to be believed.

People from northern Chile will tell you that you have no idea what *real* beauty is unless you've seen the sun rise or set over the Atacama desert. I'm prepared to take that on faith, as I do when they tell me about the rare and beautiful phenomenon of the desert bursting into flower. This happens every eight or ten years when, by some climatic freak or miracle, it rains on the world's hottest, driest desert. But, for me, it's almost always a relief, when I'm travelling south, to reach the point where the dust-brown monotony of the desert gives way to the green and fertile countryside of central Chile.

The verdure begins to appear, very gradually, in the folds between the mountains of Chile's Fourth Region above La Serena. After that, the cultivated and irrigated landscapes of central Chile become a mild visual pleasure and an antidote to the endless stony brownness of those arid regions at the northern end of the country. By the time you get as far as the rich agricultural land around Quillota and the Aconcagua river-valley north of the capital, the countryside has transformed itself into a wide, generous food-bowl that feeds the millions of Chileans who live in Santiago and provides them with an ample wine-cellar into the bargain. This part of central Chile also produces high-quality fruit, vegetables and wine for export.

But, in terms of landscape, the Englishman, like ourselves, had been most impressed by the beauty of the Chilean lake-district in the south, and especially by what was left of the rain-forests that were once the ancestral homelands of the Araucanian people. These densely-wooded, well-watered landscapes are beautifully and nostalgically celebrated in the writings of Chile's Nobel laureate, the poet Pablo Neruda, who grew up in the southern city of Temuco. Vast stretches of this richly-forested land once reached from the foothills of the Andes to the shores of the Pacific, and from the Bio-Bio river-valley to the south of the archipelago of Chiloe. It bred and sheltered the fighting Araucanian warriors who presented governors like Ambrose O'Higgins and other colonial administrators with recurring 'pacificatory' challenges and headaches. But comparatively little of those great native forests survives now, although the timber industry is still an important, if somewhat conflictive, part of the economy in the south of Chile.

Beside us, as we waited to board the *Tierra del Fuego*, a teacher with a wind-fluttered map was showing a group of students the ins and outs of the territory we'd be passing through during the first phase of our voyage. After a while we began to listen in.

'Here, to the south, immediately after we leave Puerto Montt,' he put his finger on the map, 'are the various islands of the Chiloe archipelago. La Isla Grande, the big island, and most of those smaller ones are inhabited, or else they're used for cultivation and grazing. But after we leave Chiloe behind us we'll be moving into a much bleaker landscape. All these islands are uninhabited, and around them are the wild sea-channels of Patagonia.'

This complex stretch of islands and channels, once the territory of fishing people like the Chonos, and sea-nomads like the Alacalufes, would continue nearly all the way as far as Puerto Natales, he said. At that point we'd have to disembark and cross about two hundred kilometres of steppeland in order to reach the city of Punta Arenas on the edge of the Magellan Straits.

'Chile is an extraordinary country,' the Englishman commented to the teacher, 'a long, thin ribbon of land whose southern end is almost exactly the opposite of its northern one – dry burning desert and frozen polar ice.'

'A geographical absurdity,' the teacher agreed. '*Una loca geografía* is how one of our Chilean writers described it, and I'd say he got it about right. It has everything except equatorial swamps and steaming jungles.'

We listened again while he explained, mainly for our benefit, that Chile, not content with possessing a spectrum of changing climates and territories running all the way from the heat of the Atacama desert to the foggy cold of Cape Horn, had added a few other interesting geographical odds-and-ends to its national territory over the decades since it got its independence.

'The Chilean flag flies over this little spot out here. That's Juan Fernandez, better known as Robinson Crusoe's Island.' He pointed to the tiny archipelago. 'It's nearly four hundred kilometres off the coast but it's part of the province of Valparaíso.'

'And you know that our national flag flies over this little outpost too?' He put his finger on another small black dot on the map in the one of the bluest and emptiest stretches of the South Pacific. 'European explorers called it Easter Island, but its proper name is Rapa Nui, a mysterious pocket of Polynesian culture sitting all by itself out there, three thousand kilometres from the coast of Chile, and thousands of miles away from any of the other Polynesian islands that share the same kind of culture.'

'And, of course, we also own a slice of the continent of Antarctica that reaches as far as the Pole at one end, and has a real tail at the other...'

The Englishman checked his map. 'Yes, it actually has a tail made up of islands.' He showed it to me in his guide-book.

I asked him if he had ever heard the Chilean explanation for the oddity of their country's long, thin, ribbon-shape and the curiosities of its climates and geographic variations. He shook his head. So I told him what Rebecca, with a certain amount of wry Chilean self-mockery, had told me.

'When God finished creating the world, he found that he had bits and pieces of nearly everything left over. 'What am I going to do with all this?' he asked himself. Then he had an idea. He swept up all the bits and pieces, stuck them together and dropped them down, end-to-end like crazy paving, between the Andes and the Pacific. After that he rolled down his shirts-sleeves, washed his hands, and said, 'There's Chile for you.'

The Englishman laughed. 'It sounds like what Pablo Neruda said about the Pacific,' and he read me a few lines from his guide-book:

The Pacific Ocean was in danger of falling off the map. There was nowhere to put it. It was so big and disorderly and blue it wouldn't fit in anywhere. So they came along and dropped it outside my window...

'If you walk along the shore at Isla Negra near Neruda's house, you'll see how absolutely true to life that is,' he assured me.

'And if you climb one of the hills of Valparaíso,' the teacher put in, 'and look out from another of Neruda's brilliantly-situated houses – the one he called *La Sebastiana* – you'll see the same big, moody, blue ocean, and other wonderful panoramas of Pacific scenery as well.'

'Yes,' the Englishman said, 'This Neruda of yours was quite a celebrant of nature.'

'And a dedicated eulogiser of wine, women, love, old ships, poor people, exploited workers, unusual houses, strange landscapes, wild seascapes, forests, deserts, cities, mountains, distant places, homely objects, exotic seashells.... and he had a wonderful abundance of words, images, verses, songs and stories to celebrate them with too,' the teacher finished in a burst of eloquence, during which his map nearly blew away altogether.

The *Tierra del Fuego* eventually weighed anchor and we left the little harbour at Angelmó in Puerto Montt shortly after four o'clock on a warm bright February afternoon. With the city behind us, we headed south across the Gulf of Reloncaví. Sailing conditions were nearly perfect. For a few hours we made our way through waters that were as peaceful and unruffled as the surface of an inland lake on a calm summer's evening. We stayed within sight of the coasts of the Chiloe islands for several hours. The archipelago passed us brokenly on the right, while a long, indented stretch of the Chilean mainland, which had a range of the snowy Andes towering away behind it, stayed with us on our left.

For me those island-landscapes – the distant Andes apart – looked comfortingly familiar. Chiloe was a place of small green fields, rocky cliffs, isolated houses, and little villages that clustered around sheltered fishing coves. The main difference between this green rainy part of southern Chile and the west of Ireland was that here most of the houses were made of wood rather than stone. The *alerce* of the Chilean rain-forest is a durable building material that outlasts by many centuries the people who use it to build their houses. The tree is said to take anything up to a thousand years to mature, and as many more to finally crumble away.

We met several small, brightly-painted boats making their way home to the islands after the day's fishing. Most of them were painted a vivid yellow with a luminous stripe of red above the waterline. They looked different, heavier maybe but also more colourful, than the tarry black curraghs I remembered from my childhood in Ireland. On the other hand the sea here looked darker and more mountain-shadowed than the open waters of the Atlantic.

That evening I made a nostalgic note in my journal:

> And always the heart seeks likenesses. Here it's islands, hundreds or maybe thousands of them. Clew Bay on a jagged, rocky extension, a rugged thrust for eternity? Headlands like Mulranny and Achill, peaks rising and plunging back into the dark, cold waters. The Killary and Doolough winding towards some tortuous, shadowy infinity?
>
> But this is the Chilean south, one of the remotest parts of the earth. We're almost into Patagonia now. So why

does it insistently ring up for me my own first places? Bunowen. Sitting with my father's coat wrapped around me, looking out across the Atlantic from Derrylahan on a spring day. Staring at the dark hump of Maolán, a bald rock in the ocean somewhere between Roonagh and Clare Island. Watching the great breakers cresting and foaming. Straining for a glimpse – impossible at that distance – of the nesting seabirds.

That was our wild Mayo coast on a windy day when my father sowed potatoes in a field that sloped down to cliffs that were sprayed all winter by the Atlantic. And these are the uninhabited channel-regions of Patagonia, the former home of sea-nomads, the hardy tribes who lived for centuries on these stormy coasts but have disappeared forever now. Will my people disappear like that too? *Solo Dios sabe…* only God knows.

For the rest of the evening, until darkness came on, we were sailing within sight of that broken, mountainy coastline to the east, and a scatter of small islands to the west. But when we woke up the next morning we were in a different world:

This strange, bleak, desolate seascape – the silent remoteness of these endless islands and channels – is not easy to describe. I don't think I've ever been anywhere quite as remote and bleakly beautiful as this before. It's as if we were on a distant, desolate and only vaguely familiar – but extremely watery – planet.

An endless, unchartable multiplicity of small islands and rocky humps in the sea keeps passing us by, without number or tally, on either side of the ship. Some of them are, or once were, wooded. The remnants of dead trees and old weathered stumps survive in gaunt skeletal shapes, but most of these little islets are just sheer bald lichened rock.

The blue-grey, turquoise, deep-violet, brown and inky-black shades that chase each other along the slopes and peaks that rear up as sudden cliffs, bare hills, and towering mountains are reflected eerily again in the shadowy depths below. A whole range of snow-capped Andes, or maybe just some lesser branch of the Cordillera, seems to be trying to submerge itself here, plunging and re-surfacing time and again, among these cold, deep waters.

One high, rocky formation that we passed towards sunset was like a black beetling wall that towered menacingly above the ship. We seemed to sail straight into it and then – thankfully – out under the massive overhanging rocky ledge.

As our ship made its way cautiously southwards through the umpteenth narrow channel between these uninhabited islands, we must have turned due west at some point because, for ten minutes or so, we found ourselves sailing into a strange fiery sunset. The lower half of the sky was filled with a great rack of black burning clouds, and the water in places looked as if it might suddenly catch fire. Then, just as we broke through into what were to prove more open coastal waters, we passed a lighthouse standing on a lonely headland. It looked like a strange, solitary sentinel guarding the entrance to the lonely unpeopled islands and channels that we had been sailing through all day.

'Is it a manned lighthouse, I wonder?' Rebecca said, thinking about her father and his younger days in the naval service. In Chile the navy has responsibility for every essential marine service on the country's immensely-long coastline. This includes maintaining thousands of beacons, buoys and lighthouses, as well as regular coastguard stations, naval bases and reserved docks.

'Probably not anymore. But they must have had to man light-stations like it in the past. Imagine having to do duty for months on end in an isolated place like this!'

'Once, when we were very small, my father was away from home for two years,' Rebecca said, 'though not on light-keeping service. They sent him to England for a training course. My mother was left alone with us three small ones all that time. Life in a navy family wasn't easy.'

'But she was proud of him all the same, the navy being *la crema de la crema* in Chile, as you've often told me!'

Rebecca laughed. In Valparaíso the navy is the next best thing to God – not only a source of security and protection, but also an unfailing provider, employer and paymaster for generations of families who have lived in the old seaport. Still, when we talk about her native city I like to remind Rebecca that it was an Irishman, Ambrose O'Higgins, who gave Valparaíso its first city council, and promoted it as an important commercial port at the end of the eighteenth century. And it was his son Bernardo who made it famous as the base of Chile's first national fleet, a tiny handful of ships, most of them taken in battle from the Spaniards in the early decades of the nineteenth century. The grateful people of Valparaíso named one of the most prominent hills in the city after the elder O'Higgins, Cerro Baron, which is dominated by the church of Saint Francis, probably one of the most famous landmarks in the old seaport.

Towards nightfall on our second day out from Puerto Montt, we got a taste of what rougher sailing conditions might be like. The going had been nearly perfect up until then, but, almost without warning, the sea turned rough and the ship began to ride a series of deepening swells. The weather, to all appearances, was practically the same as when we had started out from Puerto Montt. There was hardly an evening breeze to begin with, but as twilight came on, the ship began to pitch and roll very heavily. There were pale faces in the half-light on deck. Most of us hung around and put off going to bed for as long as we could, but as the night deepened and the rolling of the ship only seemed to get worse, we eventually took to our berths.

From side to side of my upper-tier bunk I rocked and swayed and hung on for dear life as I had never had to do in bed before. The carefully tucked-in bedclothes gradually worked themselves loose. After a while they were neither a help nor a comfort, and only very fitfully a covering. Towards dawn I dozed off for a while out of sheer fatigue, and I had the sensation – a very vivid one – of being back in my cradle in Bunowen where someone was rocking me from side to side with a vigorous hand.

The stretch of water we were crossing that night has a particular reputation among those who know the channel routes through Chilean Patagonia. On maps nowadays it appears as El Golfo de Penas, but the Gulf of Troubles or even the Gulf of Torments was how it was described on the maps and ships' logs of English mariners in former centuries, and apt names they were too. I read the following account of it in an old book called *Adventure and Exploration in South America*:

> Nearly eight hundred miles of the southern portion of the coast of Chile between Cape Horn in latitude 56.S. and Puerto Montt in latitude 42.S. is protected by innumerable islands; and navigation among them, though not everywhere practical for large vessels, reveals scenery of incomparable grandeur in which snow-capped mountains, glaciers, virgin forest, and rugged rock,

combine to produce effects whose majesty and extension are nowhere else to be found.

The climatic conditions, however, are about as bad as they could be; it is a region of great gales and wet, cold weather which often endures for weeks on end. There are one or two places in which the continuity of the chain of islands is broken, leaving the mainland fully exposed to the fury of the oddly-named 'Pacific' Ocean. One of these gaps is the dreaded Golfo de Penas....

The night we sailed through the waters of this wild Gulf was about the only really bad passage we had during our voyage. I was afraid that at any moment I might be pitched out of my high bunk and land on the floor below. At the same time I didn't want to climb down in case I might be hammered against the struts or knocked around on the hard floor of the cabin for the rest of the night.

I thought a lot during those long, uncomfortable hours about the eighteenth-century midshipman John Byron, grandfather of the English poet Lord Byron. He and a handful of his shipmates made a crossing through the dangerous waters of this Gulf in far more terrible conditions than we did, nearly two and a half centuries before us.

Byron was a junior officer on a vessel called *The Wager*. The ship was part of a privateering squadron of the Royal Navy commanded by Lord George Anson. These ships sailed out from Portsmouth in England in 1741 to raid Spanish ports in South America and make as much trouble as possible for Spanish shipping wherever they might come across it. The squadron's method of action was the dubious privateering practice of carrying off 'prizes,' which meant capturing ships and afterwards ransoming their crews and passengers. The overall objective was to challenge and eventually break the naval dominance of the Spaniards in the South Seas.

But *The Wager* was an unlucky vessel. She had a difficult captain or maybe just an unfortunate one. A violent storm drove her off course along the southern coasts of Tierra del Fuego when she was about to round Cape Horn, and she became separated from the rest of Lord Anson's squadron. Trying to stay on course for their next agreed meeting point, off Valdivia on the coast of Chile, the battered *Wager* was driven on to a wild rocky shore and wrecked along the Pacific coast of Patagonia.

Most of her crew survived, but when they found themselves marooned for weeks on a barren, unfrequented coast without hope of rescue, they mutinied, all except a small handful of officers and men, including young Byron, who stayed with the captain. The mutineers commandeered the ship's longboat, salvaged whatever stores they could recover from the wreck, and made off back around Cape Horn. They eventually reached the coast of Brazil and from there managed to make their way back to Europe. Meanwhile, the captain and his few remaining companions were left behind in Patagonia, on one of the most barren and inhospitable seacoasts in the world.

I must have read scores of descriptions of shipwrecks in my time, but very few of them – even Captain Bligh's memorable journey in the longboat of *The Bounty* – could match the harrowing experiences described in John Byron's account of how he and his companions survived, and eventually made their way back to England through Chiloe, Valparaíso, Santiago, and around Cape Horn again to Europe in a French frigate. Their struggle for survival in the wilds of Patagonia was a time full of horrific experiences. The most terrible sufferings of all came while they were trying – starved, vermin-infested, freezing and half-naked – to cross the snowy Gulf of Troubles in the open canoes of a nomadic Patagonian sea-tribe called the Alacalufes, who came to their aid.

The night Rebecca and I sailed through the same stormy Gulf, in summer, in our solid, steel-hulled cargo ship the *Tierra del Fuego*, I began to think with new respect about those hardy seamen of earlier times. Whether they were Englishmen or Spaniards, pirates or whalers, skilled mariners or half-naked Chilean sea-nomads, they were men of courage, endurance, and immense skill who took the hazards of these treacherous waters as part of their working life. That night I also came to the conclusion that the dark moody genius of Lord Byron, the poet, came to him from no ordinary ancestral stock.

On the evening of 3 February, our ship dropped anchor for a few hours off a tiny settlement in the middle of a watery nowhere called Puerto Eden. We had been told that here we would see one of the last surviving outposts of the Alacalufe people. These were the sea-nomads who helped the crew of *The Wager* to survive the worst experiences of their Patagonian shipwreck in the 1740s.

The Alacalufe people lived for centuries in these remote islands and sea-channels, fishing and travelling around in small portable canoes made from lashed planks or hollowed-out tree-trunks. In their tiny craft they also carried fire because without it they could never have survived in these intensely-cold and almost permanently-rainy latitudes. But the Alacalufes, it was clear from this small, isolated settlement in Puerto Eden, have disappeared almost completely as a distinctive people. Only a handful of them survive, and practically none are of unmixed blood, though their dark complexions and characteristic features were easy to pick out among the mixed population of the settlement.

Puerto Eden subsists around a naval base for the maintenance of lighthouses and other navigational services.

Lime quarries in the vicinity, and the age-old activities of fishing and harvesting the produce of the sea, seem to be the other main staples of life in the settlement. Its isolation among these uninhabited islands and remote sea-channels in the heart of Patagonia seems almost absolute. The Navimag shipping company provides its main commercial supply link with the outer world. But there has been talk recently of promoting it as a port-of-call for tourist cruisers marketing 'spectacular scenery among the unspoilt reaches of the Patagonian wilderness'.

Our ship dropped supplies – vegetables, fruit, meat, spirits, and a large box of videos for the navy. Sacks of dripping shellfish and crates of congrio, corvina, crabs and other coveted south Chilean seafoods were loaded into the refrigerated section of the *Tierra del Fuego*. That night there was an impromptu party on deck. Fillets of fish were fried, and shellfish were baked or steamed. Generous quantities of fresh bread were produced from the ship's galley, and demijohns of wine circulated freely. Most of the passengers joined in the fun.

As passengers we were a mixed lot, ranging from the respectable and elderly like our English friend, at one end of the scale, to the youthful, bohemian, weather-toughened backpackers at the other. Several of the younger passengers looked as if they were veterans of longer and rougher voyages. The two groups who stood out most clearly were the *mochileros* and the *camioneros*, backpackers and truck-drivers, respectively.

The backpackers seemed to hail, if not from every nation under the sun, then certainly from quite a few different climates and continents. Their weather-beaten complexions, peeled noses, blistered lips and sunburned limbs – and the towels, pots, frying-pans, pairs of boots, and other odds and ends dangling from their kits – suggested an ease and experience with *al fresco* travel that was daunting even to *think* about for some of the rest of us.

The truck-drivers were mostly Chileans, hardy and sometimes solitary-looking men who regularly made the journey from the country's northern desert towns, or from Santiago, to the edge of the Magellan Straits. On these trips they might clock up as many as four or five thousand kilometres, one way. So these few days on shipboard were a sort of rest-period. They slept, smoked, chatted, played cards, and spent long hours leaning over the ship's rail, gazing at the frothy wake the *Tierra del Fuego* raised among the shadowy Patagonian waters. Some of them handed around little cards offering us 'family accommodation' in Puerto Natales or Punta Arenas. Shipboard lore had it that they often had two or three households to maintain along their regular routes. It was a lonely life that generated its own compensations and complications.

The backpackers spent several hours each day stretched out on some sunny or at least sheltered part of the deck to catch up on their sleep. They were travelling in what the shipping company euphemistically described as pioneer class. This meant spending the night in *butacas* or mildly-reclinable Pullman seats in a dim, downstairs lounge near the galley. It was definitely not a comfortable way to make a long journey, but most of these seasoned young travellers seemed to know how to slough off the worst of its discomforts. Watching them catching forty winks on deck, and doing exercises to take the ruck out of their curved limbs after a night in the Pullman lounge, I learned to appreciate my top-tier bunk for the horizontal luxury it really was.

'What are you writing?' a young German girl called Gret asked me one morning as I was sitting on a quiet corner of the deck, watching the world and the islands go by. She was one of the more bleached and weather-beaten of the backpackers and had passed me a few times in this quiet spot where I was sitting with my back to a capstan. My notebook was open on my lap. It was a place where I could write my journal and enjoy the scenery in almost total peace. She peered curiously over my shoulder.

'Nothing much,' I said. 'A sort of log of the journey. Bits and pieces that strike me,' I shrugged. 'And one or two things I'm trying to work out. Personal conundrums.' But I didn't elaborate.

The truth was that during most of the voyage I had found myself avoiding the thought of finalising my decision about leaving my religious community in Ireland. It would be waiting for me as soon as I got back to Valparaíso again. This bit of unfinished business from my transition between Ireland and Chile had been very much on my mind when I left Valparaíso to begin this journey to Patagonia in January and it tended to come into my thoughts every time I sat down to write my journal. I usually dealt with it by putting it out of my mind as if it were a bad thought, but this morning I had given it a few lines in my notebook.

'You must read Christa Wolf,' Gret said suddenly, and pulled a dog-eared paperback out of her jeans pocket. It had a German-language title.

'I'll look for a translation,' I said, though without much enthusiasm. From where I was sitting at that moment on the deck of the *Tierra del Fuego* sailing through the sea-channels and uninhabited islands of Patagonia, I felt light-years away from the world of Christa Wolf. And the Berlin Wall, which had come down a few months earlier, might as well have been on another planet.

When Gret moved away, I looked at what I had written before she arrived:

This scenery calls for words from the poetics of another era. Terms like grandeur, immensity, remoteness, majesty, sublimity, imposing heights, fathomless depths, snowy peaks, and shadowy infinities come to mind – and even fens, crags, rocky fastnesses, crevasses and precipices…

Now and again a penguin or a pair of them – or very occasionally a little shoal – comes dipping by, domesticating with shiny duck-like heads and odd little bobbing movements, the isolated expanses of these dark mountain-shadowed waters.

On the face of it, this should be an ideal place to think clear thoughts about my past and future, and especially about the next step I must take in order to settle properly into this new country and life that I've chosen. But I find myself avoiding the thought of all that, for the moment, as if it were the plague.

It would be a kind of sacrilege to spend these strange beautiful days wrestling with intangibles like past and future. The peace and beauty of this great natural world might pass me by, and that would be a loss that no amount of perplexed thinking could ever compensate me for.

So I closed the notebook and sat back to look at the islands and the dark waters gliding past, like a reel from some strange silent film that I couldn't, or wouldn't, want to stop. I thought of the Magellan Straits and the island of Tierra del Fuego still ahead of us, and the wide watery wilderness of Patagonia all around us. Decisions about the future, however important, would have to wait until I got back to Valparaíso. There wasn't much I could do about them down here anyway.

7

MAGELLAN'S WORLD

We reached the little town of Puerto Natales on a chilly February evening towards dusk. The *Tierra del Fuego* sounded a few unmusical blasts on her horn as she came to the end of her long journey from Puerto Montt. She moved slowly across the waters of Last Hope Sound, swung carefully around and reversed up to the ramped berth that was her regular docking point on the waterfront in Puerto Natales. Along the edges of the Sound we could see flocks of black-necked swans, and behind them a little grey town of weather-beaten houses and rainy-looking streets. We were less than 250 kilometres now from the Straits of Magellan and would have to finish our journey across the steppes to Punta Arenas by bus.

It was strange, after those long, dream-like days of sailing through the uninhabited islands and wild landscapes of Patagonia, to find ourselves suddenly in an ordinary small city again, not quite at the southern tip of the continent, but fairly close to it, and very near the Chilean border with Argentina. I wrote in my journal:

> Incredible to find the world inhabited – deep in the heart of Patagonia! This is a small flourishing city of some 20,000 inhabitants. Sheep and cattle farming, tourism, and harvesting the age-old products of the sea, seem to be the main staples of life here. This city is the gateway to one of Chile's most beautiful national parks, Las Torres del Paine, which some years ago was designated by UNESCO as a World Biosphere Reserve.
>
> Mirella, the daughter of Rebecca's old Valparaíso friend, Raul Gonzalez, was waiting for us when the ship docked,

and ready to show us around the city when we were rested. She's a lively and well-informed guide. I look at her, thinking Rebecca might have had such a daughter. She confessed to me once that as a teenager she was keen on Raul.

I can never be sure how much Rebecca's decision not to marry had to do, in the end, with her deafness. But I suspect that her pronounced independent streak as well as a definite lack of attraction to the specifics of marriage, had even more to do with it – like myself, a sort of instinctive decision to put the energies of life elsewhere. She lasted six months as a postulant in a Santiago convent. I ploughed that particular field for thirty-three years.

We stroll through the little city that reminds me – except for its weather-beaten, grey, wooden houses – of small seaside towns in the west of Ireland when I was growing up. Gravelly, shell-strewn paths, dandelions, docks and daisies along the sidewalks, potatoes, lettuce, rhubarb, carrots and parsley in the gardens, and on the outskirts, sheep, cattle and horses grazing in small fields. We see posters on telegraph poles advertising a local rodeo. So, however far south we've travelled, we're still in Chile where the horse is a common day-labourer but also, at times, a rodeo king.

We have our lunch in a little restaurant called La Ultima Esperanza. Last Hope Restaurant! Place-names in this part of South America sometimes recall the hopes or fears or disappointments – as well as the names – of the navigators who mapped these remote coasts for European shipping. Many of them were English – Ottway, Fitzroy, Williams, Brunswick and the like.

Strains of Albinoni float softly above our heads from the restaurant's music-system. For some reason that I can't immediately identify, it reminds me of being out on the September teaching practice circuit from Carysfort years ago, supervising students in country schools, sitting in some small town drinking a cup of tea and reading the newspaper, waiting for the students' lunch-hour to be over.

A stout, well-fed Argentinian is eating at the table next to ours, and reading the local Magellanes news. (We probably look pretty well-fed ourselves now too, from over-regular eating and limited exercise on shipboard.) We figure he's an Argentinian from the way he talks to the waiter. Chileans say that Argentinians are Italians who speak Spanish and act as if they're English – even after the Malvinas War.

The food is good – a well-seasoned speciality in one of the local seafoods, quickly and courteously served. We check the bus timetable for Punta Arenas. It's hard to believe we're within about three hundred miles now of the shores of Tierra del Fuego.

A cold wind was blowing in sharp little gusts along the street near the centre of the city when we queued up at the bus station to get our tickets. It was good just to sit inside the vehicle and take shelter while it gradually filled up with passengers, and took on luggage, boxes of groceries, parcels and bundles of magazines and newspapers. The temperature was low, and the wind-chill factor sharp enough to remind us that we were now in a latitude very far south of Valparaíso.

The big, battered-looking bus was full to the doors by the time we left Puerto Natales. It was raising small clouds of dust when we reached the outskirts of the city, and much bigger ones on and off for the rest of the journey. On our map the stretch of countryside between Puerto Natales and Punta Arenas looked wide and empty. Soon the road began to twist like a dusty, grey ribbon across a stretch of bleak, treeless steppeland. We saw almost no houses or villages and very few human beings on this open landscape for long intervals at a time, but there was no scarcity at all of sheep.

Only one side of the road between Puerto Natales and Punta Arenas had been tarmacadamed on that date in February 1990, and our bus swung on and off that single narrow black-topped strip, sometimes in a hair-raising way, depending on the oncoming traffic. We'd enjoy stretches of smooth uninterrupted speed for a while, and then, with a sudden jamming on of brakes and a thud to a stand-still, or a rally-driver's careening lurch sideways, the bus would stop, or else swing over to the unpaved side of the road.

There were a couple of genuinely scary moments when, around a blind corner, another vehicle – usually a big articulated truck speeding north on its way to the ferry in Puerto Natales – appeared a few yards in front of us, using the same paved strip of the road as ourselves and heading straight for our bus at high velocity. We held our breath a few times and prayed for good reflexes for the driver. But we needn't have worried. He dipped, swerved, dodged or squeaked his way out of those looming head-on collisions every time. Still, you couldn't help having nervous thoughts about what might happen if he didn't bring it off – just once.

The big sheep-stations, called *estancias* in this part of South America, are usually located at fairly long distances from one another, so, most of the time, we saw hardly any human beings at all during our journey over the wide unsheltered steppes. People seemed to be even scarcer than the elusive ostrich-like birds called *ñandus* that we saw at intervals running into the scrub. Once or twice a solitary figure on horseback, like a still from an old movie, might catch our eye away in the distance.

We were constantly coming across huge flocks of grazing sheep, and we supposed they must be shepherded by somebody, but the way of life and farming down here certainly wasn't labour-intensive.

Even the big flocks of sheep were hardly distinguishable at a distance from the grey, scrubby surface of the steppes. There were no woolly, white dots on verdant green hillsides here, as I fondly began to remember them from Ireland. At intervals we met long trucks carrying hundreds of live animals to the ferry in Puerto Natales to be shipped north to Puerto Montt and markets farther on. I felt a twinge of sympathy for these poor cooped-up animals, just as I used to feel sad in Carysfort years ago when I saw cattle grazing the soft green pastures, munching their hapless way to the Beef Mountain in what was then called the European Common Market. In my journal I wrote:

> The sight of those poor, doomed animals in rattling mobile pens saddens me. Yesterday they had the freedom of the great windy plains of Patagonia for their roaming-ground. Today their little woolly backsides are jammed up against the mucky tailboard of a speeding truck as they travel in smelly, confined spaces towards death in some vast commercial slaughterhouse.
>
> The bus takes us deeper and deeper into the heart of a bleak windswept landscape. Short rough grasses, ferns, bracken, scrub, low, twisted, wind-sculpted thornbushes, a tiny burst of colour occasionally reminding me of a clump of Irish whins, tufts of reddish-brown grass. Sometimes a hawk or a buzzard circles slowly above some invisible prey. New-born lambs can't have it easy on these exposed steppelands.
>
> Classic Patagonia? That odd phrase stays in my mind from a tourist brochure I read recently about the south of

Argentina. I suppose this is the kind of landscape they had in mind. I'll probably never know from the inside how life really is, or was, for people living in places as remote as this. The history, boundaries, legends and geographical peculiarities of Patagonia will always remain something of a mystery to me. But from now on, at least, I'll have a vivid image of its windy plains and its vast flocks of grey, grazing sheep.

The sky turned dark and overcast as the evening and the journey wore on. Soon it was difficult to read the map or make out the names of the places we were passing in the bus. At the sight of some watery inlet we'd begin to think we must be getting near the Straits, but it wasn't so straightforward. We passed two or three promising-looking stretches of water before we finally sighted the city of Punta Arenas in the distance and knew we were coming to the end of our journey.

And then, at long last, we could see it plainly in spite of the gathering dusk, the famous Straits of Magellan, the channel that links the world's two widest oceans, the long winding navigable waterway where Ferdinand Magellan and Europe made one of maritime history's most memorable breakthroughs in the third decade of the sixteenth century.

The so-called 'discovery' of the Americas was a chapter of history I hadn't learned much about in school, and I hadn't read a great deal about it afterwards either. I knew that Columbus's celebrated landfall on the Caribbean island of Santo Domingo in 1492 had extended the horizons of Europe and was to change the life of the western hemisphere and its native peoples forever. I had a few odds-and-ends in my head too about people like Amerigo Vespucci, the Pizarro brothers, Hernando Cortes, and the conquest of Mexico and Peru, but I was unbelievably ignorant about what had actually taken place, on the ground, when Europe decided, at the beginning of the sixteenth century, that the whole of the western hemisphere was hers for the taking. I didn't even advert, I think, to the difference between an explorer and a conquistador. I thought they were probably the same sort of people.

So when I came to live in South America in the 1980s I had a great deal to learn – and a few very crucial things to unlearn – about the long and brutal process of Europe's conquest of the Americas between the fifteenth and twentieth centuries. Talking to Rebecca about the fate of the indigenous peoples of Chile – an experience of subjugation that was paralleled with far greater violence in other parts of the hemisphere – gave my learning and unlearning a more poignant edge. Comparing events that took place at opposite ends of the South American continent about the year 1520 was a case in point. It set me thinking in very concrete ways about the difference between a conquistador and an explorer, and it also forced me to recognise the almost ineluctable relationship between them, however different they might be in character, motivation, or human stature and personal qualities.

During 1520, the Spaniard Hernando Cortes, was busy in Central America plundering the country of the Aztecs and planting his country's flag with blood and fire in the territory that would later become known as Mexico. He was a conquistador of the classic stamp – brave, ruthless, gold-hungry, violent and single-mindedly ambitious for personal gain and power. Around the same time, the Portuguese navigator Ferdinand Magellan was embarking on his last and greatest voyage of exploration. Cortes was busy enriching himself at the warm and wealthy end of South America. Magellan was setting sail into some of the most unknown and dangerous seas in the world.

Magellan was Portuguese, but he made his last and greatest voyage under the patronage of the king of Spain. It had come down to a question of money in the end, as it eventually had for Columbus. The Spanish king was the only European power who was willing to back their hazardous expeditions into the unknown. The purpose of Magellan's voyage was to find a new route to the Moluccas, the so-called Spice Islands in the Far East. But his personal dream was to open up a new sea-route, one that would take him around the world and home to Europe again without ever having to turn back on his tracks. He probably had no idea how vast the world's great oceans really were. He was planning to get to the Moluccas through waters not yet traversed, much less charted, by any European navigator.

The possibility of finding a new route to the Far East was an attractive proposition for the king of Spain. His rivals, the Portuguese, were already in control of the sea-routes to the East along the coasts of Africa and around the Cape of Good Hope. Spain wanted to be independent of Portugal's far-eastern sea dominance. It also needed to chart the oceans around its own ever-expanding territories in the western hemisphere, lands that Europe had begun to think of, not so much as a paradise anymore, but as a rich and eminently-exploitable new world.

Columbus, aiming at the Indies, had never got beyond the Caribbean islands, so Magellan's voyage to the Far East, fourteen years after the great Genoese navigator's death, was still a courageous thrust into the unknown. During the first part of the exploration, several long uncertain months – in the event well over a year – would have to be spent in that most feared and difficult of all the seas known to European navigation, the stormy South Atlantic. The cold, unfamiliar southern reaches of that ocean were reported to be not only wild and dangerous, but also fearsomely unpredictable. They were seas that would test the skill and daring of navigators in far more sophisticated vessels for centuries to come.

Magellan was a navigator of genius, and he needed every skill he possessed for the challenge he had set himself now. He was a brave and unflinching commander, a tough leader with an incredibly high tolerance for uncertainty and physical hardship, a man with an unshakeable commitment to the goal he had set himself. In September 1519 he set sail from the Spanish port of Sanlucar in the Bay of Cadiz with a fleet of five ships. He headed down across the equator and then turned west into waters so wild they soon caused fear even among some of the hardiest of his captains and men. During Magellan's expedition the South Atlantic was to live up to the worst of its bad reputation.

They ran into terrifying gales, freezing fogs and treacherous currents. They suffered repeated navigational setbacks. They had injury and storm-damage inflicted on their ships, and eventually lost the *Santiago* altogether when it was wrecked off the coast of Patagonia. They endured hunger from scarce and rotting rations, knew the fear caused by intense and impenetrable fogs, put up with freezing temperatures and had dangerous brushes with the wild and rocky coasts that they had to explore minutely in search of the straits that Magellan believed – but still couldn't prove – would eventually lead them out into another ocean.

Their hardships were so great that the crew was close to mutiny several times over. One of Magellan's four remaining ships did desert him at a crucial moment during the Patagonian exploration. The *San Antonio* simply turned back to Spain one dark night and left Magellan to figure out what had happened to her. Torn between hope and fear, the remaining members of the expedition were weak, sick, hungry, dispirited, elated, bitter and angry by turns, and constantly prey to terrible fears and anxieties. They wanted to turn back to Spain, too.

But Magellan held out. Even if they had to eat the leather of the ships' fittings, he said, even if they had to eat the very rats – which eventually they did – he was determined that the expedition would sail on. On the last day of October 1520, when they were more than a year out from Spain, the battered and depleted expedition reached the entrance to a channel that Magellan called Todos los Santos because they arrived there on the Eve of All Saints. After the navigator's death this name would be changed to the Straits of Magellan, but when they woke up on that first day of November 1520 they still had no certainty that they would find a navigable outlet to an open sea at the other end of this long winding channel.

Magellan sent his ships and longboats out to explore all the likely narrows and navigable passes, including one broad and promising but ultimately disappointing opening that they afterwards bitterly named Bahia Inutil, Useless Bay. It had turned out to be another wide, watery cul-de-sac. Eventually, one of their vessels met the longed-for tidal rip, and Magellan's men sailed on with growing confidence until they reached the far end of the channel that brought them out into a different ocean and a vast new watery world.

As they sailed through into this new ocean at the western end, Magellan named the headland to the north of the Straits El Cabo Deseado, the Longed-for Cape. For reasons best known to himself – maybe because his men were more manageable now, and because any sea must have seemed an improvement on the raging South Atlantic, or because they were to find themselves becalmed in it for several weeks at a later stage in the voyage – Magellan named this new ocean the Pacific. The expedition, with only three ships left and those in a very precarious condition, headed north and west across this uncharted and apparently endless stretch of water until they eventually reached a group of islands in what was known to

Europeans – who had always come to it from the opposite direction – as the Far East.

Magellan's objective now was to carry out his commitment to the king of Spain, make a landfall on the Spice Islands, refurbish his damaged ships for the journey home, trade for a cargo of the much-coveted spices which they hoped might recoup the losses and expenses of the long voyage, and then set out again for Europe around the Cape of Good Hope and the coast of Africa. But the great navigator's health had been badly undermined by the hardships of this terrible journey. The expedition had taken over two years. He had lost men, ships and supplies, even if he hadn't lost heart. In 1521 he died as a result of an injury sustained during a skirmish between his men and the people of one of the islands where his ships were temporarily harboured.

It remained for Magellan's second-in-command, Juan Sebastian El Cano, to bring the battered expedition home again to Spain. But what was left of it now was only a pitiful remnant. Of the three ships that reached the Spice Islands only one fragile vessel, under tattered rigging, struggled back into the Gulf of Cadiz in autumn 1522. There were no more than eighteen of the expedition's original 237 members on board when the battered *Victoria* made her way up the river as far as Seville on 8 September, three years after the expedition had first set out from Sanlucar.

They got no hero's welcome. Some of them even found it hard to get their pay or their pension afterwards. Even so, Magellan and his men had proved beyond a doubt to many still-doubting Europeans that, in a round world, the further you travelled away from home, the more likely you were, after a certain point, to be on your way back. More crucially from the point of view of pragmatic people like the king of Spain, they had discovered the location of the Straits which were to serve European shipping and commerce in good stead for centuries to come.

Magellan belonged to one of the world's great traditions of maritime exploration – the Portuguese were among the most adventurous and successful navigators in European history. He shared with his contemporaries – the other explorers and adventurers who set out from the Iberian peninsula during its celebrated age of discovery and expansion – the qualities of courage, leadership, toughness, perseverance, and an immense tolerance for privation and physical hardship. However, he was clearly a man of very different calibre and stature from those who made their names by plunderering Central and South America.

Rapacious *conquistadores* like Cortes and the Pizarro brothers would violently destroy the most advanced civilisations in the Americas – the Maya, Aztec and Inca cultures – for power, greed and personal gain. They cared very little about the expansion of human knowledge or the charting of new geographical frontiers except insofar as these opened up further prospects of wealth and plunder. Explorers like Magellan, on the other hand, who ventured into new seas, mapped unfamiliar coasts, and pushed beyond the limits of their known world – although they were tough and ruthless on occasion too – were men of an essentially different stamp. Even the historical and cultural revisionism of the twentieth century, with its understandable scepticism about 'discoverers,' conquerors and colonisers, has had to treat them with respect. Paradoxically, of course, Magellan may have been fortunate to meet his death in the Far East. It saved him from becoming too closely identified with the destructive and inhuman side of the Iberian expansionist wave of which he was also inescapably a part.

Sometimes Rebecca refers to the Spaniards who conquered Central and South America in the sixteenth century as *ladrones*, *puros ladrones*, robbers and nothing more. It seems a harsh judgement on people whom Europe would look on as pioneers and fearless adventurers for centuries to come. But history, even as the Spaniards themselves recorded it, bears out the dark and cruel side of the conquest of the New World to a horrifying degree. The warm lands from the Caribbean coasts as far south as central Chile were seized and plundered, and their natural wealth greedily exploited by the soldiers and colonists from Europe. At the same time, the indigenous inhabitants were subjected to a violence and servitude so bitter that the memory of it seems to have been bred into the very bones and genes of their descendants.

The north of the continent was to prove much more tempting to the plunderers from Europe, of course, than the cold lands around the Straits of Magellan. In the north, it was relatively easy for the more unscrupulous kind of conquistador to make a quick fortune. The civilisations at that end of the continent were advanced in mining, agriculture and commerce, as well as in the working of precious metals, pottery, building, astronomy, religion and the arts of war. There was gold to be had for the taking, and further supplies of it could be mined with exploited native labour whenever the ready-made treasures ran out. In the lands formerly controlled by the warrior-aristocrats of the Maya, Aztec and Inca empires, the gold hunger of the Spaniards was fed in the beginning with vast amounts of looted treasure.

But even when the gold and silver from the treasuries and mines was reduced to a controlled flow, it was possible in those warm northern territories – where the climate was favourable and the lands, cleared with the sweat of native labour, were extensive and fertile – to make fortunes of various other kinds. In Patagonia and southern Chile, on the other hand, there was no immediate bait for Spaniards of the plundering, get-rich-quick type. The territories around the Magellan Straits were neither wealthy nor warm, and they were certainly not civilised in any then-recognised European sense of the word. Patagonia was difficult to get at. It was far away and surrounded on all sides by dangerous seas and treacherous channels. It would be centuries before anyone was able to imagine how you could possibly make a fortune there.

Still, a few Spaniards did try to set up small settlements along the Straits, for strategic reasons, during the fifteenth and sixteenth centuries. One of the most tragic of those – or possibly just one of the most unfortunate and foolish – was Pedro Sarmiento de Gamboa. He was involved in two expeditions to the far south. For the second one he mounted a highly ambitious project and persuaded King Philip II of Spain to finance an expedition to annexe the lands at either end of the Magellan Straits for the Spanish Crown.

The idea was to set up fortified settlements at strategically-selected points along the channel and so prevent other European powers from making their way freely through the Straits to menace Spanish colonies and shipping along the Pacific coast. The English privateer, Sir Francis Drake, had already made a marauding expedition – rounding Cape Horn in the process – 'to singe the beard of the king of Spain'. He had plundered and caused havoc and terror in Spanish settlements up and down the Pacific coast. He had even sacked Valparaíso which wasn't a settlement of much wealth or consequence at the time. In an old history of this city I once saw a line-drawing of Drake with a succinct caption underneath: 'A Gentleman in England – A Robber in America.'

The Spanish king had strategic reasons, as well as an eye to some possible future gain, for looking favourably on Sarmiento de Gamboa's proposition to set up fortified towns on the Magellan Straits. In 1581, he invested Gamboa with the title of Governor of the Magellan Straits, and on 25 September of that year the expedition set out from Sanlucar with a fleet of twenty-three ships. There were about 3,000 people on board, including crew-members, soldiers and would-be colonists. The naval commander of the expedition was Captain General Diego Flores. But the troubles of Gamboa's expedition began almost before he left the coast of Spain. The contracts for provisioning the ships turned out to have been subject to court patronage, intrigue and fraud. The supplies, implements and armaments were of the cheapest and most unserviceable kind. Before long, Gamboa was at odds with the Captain General, Diego Flores.

Disaster struck early. A devastating storm hit them in the South Atlantic, resulting in the loss of 800 lives and the wreck of several ships, and they were forced to turn back to Spain. But Gamboa was determined to set out again, although he now had a much smaller fleet. After a further run of misfortunes they arrived at the Magellan Straits in February 1584. Only five ships and a few hundred colonists remained to carry out Gamboa's ambitious project on these bleak shores.

The story of the expedition from there on becomes a chronicle of bickering, bitterness and despair. The records make harrowing reading. A disastrous shortage of food, a scarcity of the supplies and instruments needed to build living quarters and sow crops in a cold infertile territory, bitter divisions among the members of the expedition – the tally of their grievances and disadvantages mounted up. The most calamitous of all their quarrels led to the flight of three of Gamboa's five ships and their crews back to Spain, taking with them most of the scarce food supplies and ammunition, the life-and-death necessities of the colonists they were leaving behind.

This meant that Sarmiento de Gamboa and his remaining followers were in a truly desperate situation. But such was the folly or delusion or megalomania of the man that he insisted, against all the odds, in going ahead and trying to set up his two cities. These were tiny makeshift clusters of wooden huts behind sheltering stockades, to which he gave the grandiose names of La Ciudad del Nombre de Jesus and La Ciudad del Rey Don Felipe. They were cities by virtue of Sarmiento de Gamboa's ambitious paper-plans only, projections of an aspiring and impractical mind.

The grim reality along the Straits was the famished misery of a few hundred colonists trying to survive with almost no food supplies and only the inadequate shelter of two sets of makeshift huts, one at either end of the long, exposed channel. A more responsible and less deluded leader would almost certainly have cut his losses at that stage and tried to get his people out while he still had a pair of seaworthy ships to take them.

Instead, Sarmiento de Gamboa went on trying to build his 'cities' until one day, while he was on board the *Maria*, a calamitous storm cut the ship from her moorings and drove her out into the South Atlantic. Running before the wind for weeks, she eventually reached the coast of Brazil. There, Sarmiento de Gamboa tried to organise an expedition to supply his colonists on the Straits with some of the necessities for survival, but he failed to find any backers. Eventually, he set out for Spain to report to King Philip II and to look for more help.

But Gamboa seems to have attracted misfortune the way a carcass attracts flies. First he was captured by English privateers and held prisoner for six months. When they released him he set off for Spain again, only to fall into the hands of French Huguenots who held him hostage for two years. By the time he arrived back in Spain he had lost all credibility. Nobody wanted to hear about his colonies on the Magellan Straits, much less to send another expedition to such an unlucky territory.

As for the unfortunate colonists whom he had left behind in Patagonia, hunger and exposure soon reduced their numbers. They had no seaworthy ship and no able navigator to get them back to Spain, no seed or breeding stock or implements to make an attempt at farming, no ammunition for hunting. Their situation was hopeless. When the English privateer Thomas Cavendish anchored off the so-called City of King Don Felipe in 1587, what he found was a ghost-colony, a remnant so starved and miserable he re-named the place Puerto Hambre, the Port of Starvation.

One of the last colonists from Gamboa's expedition was rescued by another English privateer, Andrew Merrick, in 1590. He had survived in the only way possible along that desolate coast, by hunting for animals and birds, first with an arquebuss, and then when powder for the arquebuss ran out, with a bow and arrows, like the nomadic Patagonian tribes who had lived as hunters around the Straits for centuries.

The failure of Pedro Sarmiento de Gamboa to establish a Spanish settlement on the Magellan Straits in the sixteenth century was, in effect, a reprieve for the indigenous tribes of Patagonia. Although they still had occasional contacts with passing European ships – vessels sailing through the Straits to the Spanish settlements along the Pacific coast, or whaling and sealing expeditions that exploited these southern waters in increasing numbers during the eighteenth and nineteenth centuries – there would be no systematic European settlement in Patagonia until late in the nineteenth century.

Unlike the exploited peoples at the warmer end of the continent, the tribes of the far south would be able to breathe their native air freely for another few centuries. But the freedom of the southern tribes would not last indefinitely. The consequences of that initial sixteenth-century contact with the white man's civilisation – the fatal impact as it was to be called after Captain Cooke's time – were only delayed. A time-bomb had begun to tick which would eventually explode and wipe out the indigenous tribes of Patagonia.

8

MEN AND WOMEN OF THE WIND

Punta Arenas, the most important city in Chilean Patagonia, is the capital of a historic region named not for any of its original Patagonian inhabitants, but for Magellan who once touched very briefly on its shores. The region is called Magellanes. Punta Arenas is a grey, windy little city with the sharp airs, cool temperatures and changeable weathers of a north European coastal town, like some small port on the edge of the North Sea. The name, which in English means 'sandy point', first became familiar to Chileans as the location of one of the country's most isolated penal colonies, set up there early in the nineteenth century, soon after the country got its independence from Spain.

Although Chile wasn't alone in choosing distant and inaccessible places for its prison colonies, some of its choices turned out to be memorable for other reasons as well. Juan Fernandez, Robinson Crusoe's Island, was one of the far-off locations used as a prison colony after the tiny archipelago came under Chilean rule early in the nineteenth century. In more recent times, a remote coastal strip of the Atacama desert called Pisagua, formerly associated with the nitrate-mining industry, acquired a lethal notoriety during the Pinochet years because of the many political dissidents who were relegated or 'disappeared' there.

In Punta Arenas, the prison colony soon developed a violent reputation. By 1842, the original prison, a cluster of log huts inside a high wooden stockade, had been sacked by the inmates and burned to the ground twice. By 1877, it had been burned down for the third time, and there were frequent violent uprisings and escapes. Sometimes the guards, who felt they weren't much better off than the prisoners, joined the fugitives and took off into the wilds of Patagonia, especially after it began to be rumoured that there was gold in the area.

But a whole new era began in this part of South America with the advent of a European technology that changed the speed of shipping in the nineteenth century. Early in the 1880s the vessels of the Pacific Steam Navigation Company began to sail through the Straits and make regular calls at Punta Arenas on their way to such newly-booming seaports as Valparaíso and San Francisco on the Pacific coast and Buenos Aires on the Atlantic. Soon the PNSC brought Punta Arenas and the area along the Magellan Straits into regular touch with a wider world.

This new and faster means of travel and trade attracted a wave of emigrants, settlers, and business-speculators to the land around the Straits. Some were farmers who set up *estancias*, big sheep and cattle ranches from which they exported meat, wool and hides to the rapidly-growing industrial cities of North America and Europe. Their most regular outlets were through Buenos Aires and Liverpool, but they also did a growing business with cities along both coasts of the United States. The California Gold Rush, with its need to feed mushrooming populations in new cities along the North Pacific Coast, brought unexpected wealth to the farming settlers of Patagonia. These developments soon attracted bankers, builders, property speculators, shipping agents, mining prospectors and commercial entrepreneurs of many kinds to the region. Most of them found it convenient to establish themselves in or around the growing port of Punta Arenas, and the city was soon to experience its own small but lucrative boom.

The big sheep and cattle stations which came into being around the Straits at the turn of the century – especially those of the Menendez and Braun families, who saw themselves as the founding-fathers of European civilisation in Patagonia – were developed on the basis of generous land-grants from the Argentinian and Chilean governments. These struggling new states saw the possibility, for the first time, of some revenues accruing to them from their distant and undeveloped lands in the far south, so they encouraged the spread of the European settlements.

The big *estancias* rapidly became the nucleus of a new kind of life and economy in Patagonia. They introduced the ruthless efficiency of big business and export marketing into a world that was previously the domain of free-roaming nomadic hunters and fishing tribes. The discovery of alluvial gold in parts of Patagonia in the 1890s brought another wave of adventurers to the region. The scene was gradually being set for one of the most tragic chapters in the history of this part of South America.

This amalgam of progress and disaster was the story that would gradually unfold itself for Rebecca and me as we made our way around southern Patagonia during the following weeks, but on our first morning in Punta Arenas everything was bright, warm and cheerful. The temperature was in the mid-twenties, about the same as we were used to at this time of year on our local beach in Valparaíso nearly three thousand kilometres to the north. That was the first surprise. We didn't realise that we had arrived on the Straits at the beginning of an unusual summer heat-wave. We were also delighted to discover that the house where we were staying with Rebecca's friends, the Silvas from Valparaíso, was less than a hundred yards from the shore of the Straits. There was even a little pebbly beach with a good view of the harbour within a few minutes walk of the front door. I made a note in my journal that first morning:

Hard to believe we're sitting on the beach on the northern shore of the Magellan Straits, and that I have my feet in the water – cold but not freezing – of the famous channel that unites the two great oceans. The sun is hot on our backs, and there's a mild breeze offshore. Children are skimming stones, paddling and playing along the edge of the strand. The waves rise in light breaking ripples around a row of little fishing boats riding at anchor a short way out from the shore.

Moored along the docks nearly opposite us are some of the ships, including one big ice-breaker, of the Chilean Antarctic fleet. A few cargo vessels are berthed alongside them. One is like a black-and-white striped seabird. The others are dark-green and grey, but the biggest one of all is painted bright vermilion, a colour that gleams spectacularly above the ship's waterline and is reflected perfectly in the almost mirror-smooth surface below.

A single oil-rig is located close to the southern shore of the harbour. Too near the coast altogether, it seems to me, but maybe it hasn't been towed out to its working location yet. It dominates the horizon to our right where an old harbour dredger is creaking rustily under the operations of an ancient and fitfully-swivelling crane.

So this is Patagonia, and we've arrived at last on the shores of the Magellan Straits. How ordinary it all seems, and how peaceful and beautiful.

'If you start at the Magellan monument in the main plaza, you can take your bearings from there for practically anywhere else you want to go in the city,' our host Jorge advised us when we set out on our first round of city sightseeing. So we made our way to the steps of the Magellan monument, closed our guidebooks, and stood back to take a good look at the most famous landmark in Punta Arenas. This is probably the most imposing of the city's civic sculptures, though not to my mind the most memorable. That would turn out to be El Ovejero, the monument to The Sheepman with his horse and dog and flock, which we were to see later in the day.

The great navigator stood high above us on his raised pedestal gazing out, not only over the little tree-lined plaza and the streets around the centre of the city, but across the blue-grey waters of the Straits and the distant horizons of Tierra del Fuego as well. This sprightly-looking Magellan is the focal point of a group-sculpture of aspiring neo-classic pretensions. With a telescope in one hand, a cap in the other, and a long sword reaching almost to the ground beside his heel, the navigator pauses briefly to survey the Straits, like a man impatient to be on his way. Around the central plinth on which he stands, but lower down, are the massive bronze figures of some naked Patagonian Indians, symbolic figures fulfilling the role of a dominated people. One of them looks a little like the Celtic figure of the Dying Gaul. Magellan's boot rests on the barrel of a thick unfriendly-looking cannon whose blunt snout points seaward above the heads of the crouching Indians.

This expansive piece of monumental self-celebration was raised by the ranchers, bankers and successful businessmen of early-twentieth-century Patagonia, ostensibly to honour Magellan, but more surely to commemorate themselves and the handsome fortunes they were making down here at the start of the century. The Magellan depicted in this monument is a figure that the great Portuguese navigator himself might find hard to recognise. He didn't come here, after all, to dominate, much less to dispossess or exterminate the Patagonian tribespeople. When all was said and done, Magellan simply navigated the Straits like a good sea-captain, and then sailed away on his voyage and trading mission for the king of Spain.

One of the most curious legacies he left behind him was the name he gave to the ocean he found when he sailed out of the Straits on the other side and headed northwest in search of the Spice Islands. I wake up to the sight of this ocean in Valparaíso most mornings and walk along its shores almost every day. I'm nearly as familiar with its shifting moods now as I was with the Atlantic off the west coast of Ireland when I was a child, and, on the whole, Pacific is one of the last names I'd ever think of calling it. But Magellan, who sailed over great wide expanses of it in fragile ships, must have had his reasons.

Rebecca mentioned her Araucanian ancestors again this morning while we were standing on the steps of the Magellan monument. It stretches my credulity sometimes, this pure Amerindian blood of hers, considering her family-name is Perez Roldan which sounds Spanish or at least Creole enough to me. But every so often she allows herself a burst of righteous indignation about the injustices of colonial history, and the unworthy treatment meted out to her ancestors by the Spaniards, sentiments I can understand, with or without Amerindian ancestors. We found ourselves indignant, admiring and ambivalent by turns as we made our way around the city and neighbourhood of Punta Arenas.

In spite of the mildly north-European flavour of the city, there are intimations, at intervals, of ambivalence and regret about its vanished indigenous past. These are especially perceptible in the city's more reflective spaces – the museums, plazas, galleries and viewing-points that invite you to gaze out across the steppes and think about Patagonia's history. The price paid for material progress down here in the twentieth century has not only been the loss of an indigenous people with a unique way of life, but also the end of an extraordinary human relationship with one of the most challenging and inhospitable parts of the earth. The story has an inescapable sadness. The disappearance of the native tribes of Patagonia was not the consequence of a slow attrition or some gradual erosive process of history. It didn't come about as a result of armed conquest or defeat in battle by some superior military power, either. Its special poignancy lies in the fact that it happened through the supposedly-peaceful action of European settlement and commercial expansion, as recently as the beginning of the twentieth century.

In other parts of southern Chile it's still possible to meet descendants of some of the native peoples who once inhabited the land. They may be few, but there are still Mapuche Indians in the Temuco region and Pehuenches in the valleys of the Bio-Bio river. They live in their ancestral homelands and preserve their traditional ways of life, even if they don't seem to prosper much in economic terms. In recent decades they have had to live with the recurrent threat of exploitative technological projects making inroads on their lands for commercial convenience and profit. But, so far, they have managed to maintain their inherited culture and beliefs, and have a pride in their identity, while retaining some part at least of the way of life fashioned over the centuries by the wisdom of their ancestors. In Punta Arenas, however, so complete has been the disappearance of these remarkable people who were lords of the land here until the end of the nineteenth century, that the only Patagonians we saw were those bronze figures at the base of the Magellan monument.

We touched the smooth bronze toe of the Dying Gaul figure to pay tribute to these vanished people and to make a wish, as visitors to the city are supposed to do, before we moved away. For some reason the gesture reminded me of tracing the sign of the cross and opening my arms wide to renounce the devil 'with all his works and pomps', in the rite prescribed for pilgrims on the holy island of Lough Derg in the north of Ireland. The Patagonians, unfortunately, couldn't repel the aggressive European with all his self-serving works and pomps. They did their best, but survival was an option that history and the white man finally denied them. The Magellan monument in Punta Arenas is an eloquent, if unintended, testimony to that painful past.

We spent a while later that morning in the Salesian Museum which is located near the Magellan monument and close to the centre of Punta Arenas. This little museum houses an impressive collection of minutely-classified flora and fauna, fossils, physical remains, artifacts, maps, chronicles, photographs and general memorabilia of old Patagonia. It also attempts, with surprisingly colourful and vivid effects, to depict as accurately as possible what is known of the life and customs of the nomadic tribespeople who lived around the Straits in the century before they finally became extinct. Some corners of this little museum felt oddly congenial to me. Memories of childhood activities like collecting eggs, climbing trees, catching small fish, hunting rabbits, picking winkles and carrageen, gathering nuts and berries or haws and sloes, familiar things that reminded me of growing up in Bunowen in the 1940s, came flooding back to me. Old Patagonia seemed less harsh and outlandish to me after that, although there was no doubt that it was a bleak landscape and a primitive and probably crude way of life.

But a museum is a museum, and eventually we felt the need of a reviving cup of coffee. Near the café we had the good fortune to come across a small art exhibition. The pictures and drawings were by a young Punta Arenas artist called Patricio Ivelic Suarez, whose name suggested a typical latter-day regional mixture of European ethnic origins. The exhibition, which was a tribute to the life and times of the lost tribes of Patagonia, was called *Hombres del Viento*: Men of the Wind. I silently changed that to Men and Women of the Wind.

In line-drawings and charcoal sketches, some of which were strikingly personal and vivid, the young artist depicted these primitive men and women – nomads, hunters, warriors and fishing people – as he saw or imagined them. For him, they were a people who had been strong, swift and sudden like the wind. But, like the wind that once blew around them on the wide Patagonian steppes, they had disappeared, condemned, the young artist seemed to suggest, to the fate of an extinction that had been cruel, unnecessary, and avoidable. His pictures tried to evoke the wild grace, skill, speed and primitive life-force of those vanished nomads of the far south. It was an idealisation but, for me, a strangely appealing one.

During our bus journey from Puerto Natales to Punta Arenas we had seen some of the long-legged, ungainly-looking birds that are known as *ñandus* in the south of Chile. The *ñandu* is a Patagonian cousin of the emu or ostrich found in other parts of the southern hemisphere. For me it was fascinating to see just how fast those big birds could run, and even more surprising to notice how, in spite of their height and apparent awkwardness, they could hide themselves in a few seconds on that exposed plain.

The Book of Job takes time to marvel at the speed of the ostrich, though it also comments very bluntly on the apparent carelessness and foolishness of the bird. She lays her eggs and leaves them unprotected on the ground, it says. '*But even if God made her foolish/when she begins to run/she can laugh at any horse or rider.*' One of the most telling tributes paid to the hunting tribes of Patagonia, particularly the Ona and Hausch people, by the few Europeans who really knew them well, was that as foot-hunters they could outrun the *ñandu*. The bird was in some ways an image of themselves, an unprotected dweller on an exposed landscape. But the *ñandu* has survived. The tribes have disappeared.

How places like Tierra del Fuego and Valparaíso got their names was something that intrigued me when I first heard what those names meant. Nobody can say for certain why Valparaíso was ever called a 'valley of paradise', though there's no shortage of flattering and unflattering assessments of the suitability of the name. But in the case of Tierra del Fuego there is at least a likely story.

The European sailors who first saw this island from the decks of their ships noticed thick plumes of smoke rising into the cold air from the campfires of the hunting tribes, so they named it the Land of Smoke and entered this into the log of their voyage. Apparently, the king of Spain didn't like the idea of such an off-putting name for any part of his potential dominions, and he ordered the royal cartographers to change it. 'There's no smoke without a fire,' he's reported to have said, as he gave instructions for the island to be renamed and inscribed on all future maps as Tierra del Fuego, the Land of Fire. It was an improvement, certainly, on the Land of Smoke. Now that the hunting tribes are gone, the only fires visible from a distance around Tierra del Fuego are the exhaust-flames from the towers of its oil-rigs.

Although he may have taken some interest in naming the place, the king of Spain never actually established his rule over the island of Tierra del Fuego. He didn't find the effort worth his while. There was no particular profit in it, and after the failure of adventurers like Sarmiento de Gamboa to make strategic settlements on the Straits in the sixteenth century, the tribes of the south were left to their own devices for a few centuries.

The Fuegians, as Englishmen like Fitzroy and Darwin began to call the islanders early in the nineteenth century, seem to have included a number of different tribes. The Yaganes or Yamanes, southern counterparts of the Alacalufes, were sea-nomads who lived along the stormy coasts in the far south. They moved about in small boats made of lashed planks or hollowed-out tree-trunks, and they subsisted on a diet of fish, seal-meat, molluscs, algae, seabirds and anything else they could take from the sea or gather along the coast. The territories of the Yagan people were the bitterly-cold southern extremes of the continent, the coasts around the Beagle Channel and the Straits of le Maire. Incredibly, they seem to have gone practically naked in all weathers.

The Alacalufes, who were like the Yaganes, roamed much further north and sometimes made their way as far as the islands of Chiloe. They were the sea-people – reportedly rather dour and surly in their temperament – who helped to save the life of John Byron and his companions when *The Wager* was wrecked off the coast of Patagonia in 1741. Their diet, especially the raw fish and rancid seal-blubber that they ate when they couldn't kindle a fire, wasn't much to young Byron's liking, but without it he probably wouldn't have survived to become a notable sea-lord and the grandfather of a famous English poet.

The other two tribes of Tierra del Fuego, the Ona and the Hausch – related also to the Tehuelches or Selknam of Argentinian Patagonia – were land-nomads and foot-hunters. Their most prized food was the meat of the guanaco, a wild southern cousin of the alpaca and the llama which had been domesticated by the Andean peoples in Bolivia and Peru. Most of the scarce clothing and primitive camping shelters of the Patagonian tribes were made from guanaco skins.

Of all the native inhabitants of Tierra del Fuego, the Ona were reportedly the most impressive. They were tall, quick, strong and resourceful, skillful trackers and hunters with an incredible tolerance for cold and hardship, real men and women of the wind. The entire southern end of the continent was supposedly named after them by the Spaniards – Patagonia, the land of the people with big feet.

The story of how these hardy tribespeople became extinct, vanishing without a trace from the face of the earth, is a lesson to ponder as well as a tragedy to lament. It includes names that have an acclaimed place in history, men who expanded Europe's horizons, knowledge and culture, as well as people who spread its power and commerce across the surface of the globe. Magellan in the sixteenth century, Cooke and Bougainville in the eighteenth, Fitzroy and Darwin in the nineteenth, were among the forerunners, but the record also includes cartographers, naturalists, whalers, sealers, navigation companies and, in later times, missionaries, miners, ranchers, business speculators, bankers and modest emigrant settlers.

Most of these people didn't set out to displace the Patagonians from their tribal lands. Many of them were never aware of the role they might be playing in bringing about such a tragic outcome, but towards the end of the nineteenth century some certainly were. The big ranchers or *estancieros*, in particular, knew what was happening, but they still pressed forward with the wholesale acquisition of the tribal lands. Intent on making, not just a living, but the largest commercial profits possible out of the ancestral hunting-grounds of the Patagonians, they were among the protagonists of one of the saddest chapters in the history of Europe's arbitrary and selfish dealings with the native peoples of the western hemisphere.

Latter-day Punta Arenas enjoys the amenity of a government-sponsored duty-free shopping zone which is located on the outskirts of the city. This is one of several incentives designed to make southern Patagonia more attractive or at least less expensive to live in, especially for the professional people who are needed to operate the public services at such an immense distance from the seat of central government in Santiago. Chile's other big duty-free shopping zone is in Iquique on the edge of the Atacama desert in the far north.

Rebecca was keen to do some duty-free shopping for her confectionery business, but I was lukewarm about the prospect. In the end I went with her to see what the Zona de Libre Comercio looked like. When we got off the bus outside the big neon-lit complex I spotted a signpost for a small local museum. It was an outdoor heritage centre dedicated to the life of the early European settlers in Patagonia. That theme gave me pause for a minute. But in a choice between the out-of-doors, and spending time in a shopping centre, I'll take the open-air option any time.

So I left Rebecca in the duty-free centre with her shopping-list, and made my way down the road to spend a while wandering around among the restored farmhouses, old machinery, and random memorabilia of the first people who succeeded in making Patagonia productive in farming. I was glad afterwards that I did. Most of those early emigrant settlers were hard-working men and women who faced enormous challenges, and succeeded against heavy odds. They had to overcome the hardships of a bleak territory, a cold climate, immense distance from their original homes and families, and the sheer physical labour of putting a new life together in a windy, uncomfortable, uncultivated and faraway land. That they succeeded in making this desolate part of the world productive and to some degree hospitable was no small achievement. My only quarrel with them – though it was a fundamental one – was that they didn't do this without being implicated, some of them very directly it seems, in the disappearance or actual extermination of Patagonia's indigenous people. Some form of peaceful co-existence with the native inhabitants of the land must surely have been possible.

The museum was located in a pleasant little park which was part of the campus of the University of Magellanes. The fresh pastoral back-drop to the exhibits was one of the things I liked most about it. Wandering around a wide field with soft summer grass underfoot, you could examine the old machinery, wagons, sheds and implements that were used to turn this wild land into a relatively profitable and productive region. In the reconstructed houses you could see how these men and women had tried to re-create some of the small conveniences that they had left behind them in Europe, comforts which they certainly weren't going to find on the steppes of Patagonia. The people who lived here before them weren't into comfort or domestic convenience.

Elsewhere, there were old farm carts with rusting iron hoops, horse-drawn mowing machines with long wooden shafts, buggies and wagons with thin rubber tyres. It was strange to think that these old carts and horse-drawn wagons were the forerunners of the immense articulated trucks we had met on our bus journey across the steppes, the great juggernauts in which animals and farm products are transported to market over the wide plains of Patagonia nowadays. The drovers and wagon-drivers of a hundred years ago had to be a hardier race of men.

Before I went back to join Rebecca, I sat under a tree at the edge of the field and made a note in my journal:

> The fragrance of wild roses is drifting in from a hedge behind me, and I'm sitting in the airy shade of a mountain ash, the tree that in Irish mythology bore the bewitched fruit, *na caortha caorthainn*. There are clovers and cowslips, daisies, dandelions, buttercups and soft summer grasses all around me.

This landscape even has its own version of gorse, a rough broom as bright with yellow blossoms as whins on the side of a ditch in springtime in Ireland. There's also something that looks like an Irish hawthorn – how very much at home he must have felt here – I think suddenly of my father's old neighbour from Bunowen who came to Patagonia and died in Buenos Aires more than forty years ago.

Sitting in the shade, with a soft thick bank of summer clover around me and the fragrance of new-mown hay drifting in from a nearby field, I find myself searching for a four-leaved clover as I used to do in Bunowen when I was small. And I feel my good fortune in being here, enjoying the summer sunshine in a place that looks like the west of Ireland but is actually on the coast of Patagonia.

Rebecca emerged from the shopping-centre some time later, laden down with purchases. 'We'll have to come back here,' she announced straight away, 'at least once more before we go back to Valparaíso. The prices are too good to miss.' I thought with a flicker of resignation about the extra weight another round of shopping was going to add to our already oversized luggage.

An odd little entry in my journal that evening recorded something that happened while Rebecca was having a siesta to recover from her shopping exertions, and I was sitting alone in the living-room:

The room where I'm sitting to write is shady and cool. The wide ground-floor window looks out on the street and then across the waterfront to the harbour and the Straits… But suddenly I'm conscious of being watched. This is, after all, the house of a detective-inspector, and at this moment he's on a round trip of nearly 2,000 kilometres chasing a bank-fraud and cattle-thief, a big-time crook who set up a clever scam involving bank accounts in Puerto Montt and Punta Arenas, and a recently-purchased herd of cattle that disappeared suddenly over the border into Argentina.

The man who's looking in the window goes through the motions of combing his hair and using the window as a mirror. He peers intently through the middle pane, runs the comb through his hair, slicks it back with his hand, looks in again, pockets the comb, and then moves on – much to my relief.

It could be as simple as that, a man combing his hair and using the first window he passes as a mirror. But it needn't be... I hope I'll never find out.

A beautiful white ship, like one of the great passenger-liners in my grandfather's picture books, but without the distinctive old tilting smoke-stacks, appeared suddenly in the Straits that evening while we were having our supper – a luxury-liner on a world cruise. We watched it moving slowly across the line of the horizon and then dropping anchor at a chosen point far out beyond the enclosed waters of the harbour. Too big for the docks, or staying here too briefly, it didn't come in to berth. There's a launch-service for passengers who want to come ashore.

After supper we went for a stroll along the seafront to get a better look at the big cruiseship. An evening breeze sprang up suddenly and cut in sharply from the Straits. An old man with a canvas sack slung over his shoulder was scavenging in a bin, fingering through a stinking box of discarded shellfish, looking for a handful of food to salvage. The first pairs of silvery-haired tourists from the cruiseship came through the harbour-gates, swinging their cameras. One of them was already getting her lens focussed to take a picture, to catch the local colour, get a flavour of life in the most southerly city in the world. The old man shuffled uneasily away.

Three small boys stood sharing out pesos on a corner near the harbour wall. The transaction had something to do with the sale of fish or shellfish. The sharing looked like an intricate business and there was obviously a great deal of satisfaction in it. All that counting out, stacking, watching, fair-shares, and the pleasure of the anticipated spending. They sauntered off towards the town-centre, jingling the coins in their pockets, their expressions anonymously memorialised in the snapshots of at least two sets of passengers from the big white cruiseship.

Magellan, looking out from his pedestal in the plaza, must take some satisfaction in the advances shipping has made since his day, especially when a gleaming white seabird like this one perches on the horizon. No frail, storm-tossed bark to carry these latter-day children of good fortune around the globe, no plaything at the mercy of unpredictable winds and weathers. And yet it's not hard to imagine that, in a different mood, these coasts and currents could still make life uncomfortable even for such a great white cruise-ship and its passengers.

We were going on an excursion the following day along the coast to see the breeding-habitats of the penguins. As we turned home for the night the big ship in the bay lit up suddenly like a gigantic twin-peaked floating Christmas tree. They were celebrating a gala evening on the Straits before moving on the next day – heading for where? The South Pacific? Easter Island? Tahiti? Hawaii? Or up the Atlantic coast to Buenos Aires and on to Rio where it would soon be carnival-time?

Maybe it was just as well the Patagonians bowed out while their wild strength and primitive dignity were still intact, I thought suddenly. Men and women of the wind, how could they escape being corrupted and diminished by our easy and frivolous life-ways? Like that Aymara man in Bolivia who, all unknowingly, posed an unanswerable question for me once. He had carried his sick wife to hospital on an improvised seat strapped to his back, and had struggled along the edge of a gaping ravine through most of one hot day and part of a freezing Andean night. I was left with the question:

An ambulance, a roadway?
Good treatment for your wife?
Necessary imperatives of civic progress,
but what can progress ever give you
that will not be incomparably less
than what you have, what you already are,
dwarfing us, our bought conveniences?

The following morning we woke up to another hot sunny day in Punta Arenas. The Straits looked as calm and unruffled as the peaceful waters of an inland lake. Even the grey streets of the little city seemed to catch a summer glow from the clear skies and unclouded horizons all around us. It was a perfect day for our visit to the breeding-grounds of the penguins.

We lined up to buy our tickets at a small agency that organised minibus excursions to Las Pingüineras on the coast some miles north of Punta Arenas. It was mid-morning but already the sun felt oppressively hot considering the latitude we were in. We had long since decided that we probably weren't going to find much use for the jackets and sweaters we had packed before starting out from Valparaíso. All the rainwear, the changes of shoes, the woolly jumpers and padded parkas had turned out to be just a bulky nuisance. Either we were exceptionally fortunate with the weather, or the hole in the ozone-layer needed to be taken more seriously.

'I suppose we should just count our blessings and stop complaining about the heat,' Rebecca said virtuously, but then she wiped her brow and said, *'Pero, Dios mio, que calor!'*

We had certainly been enjoying the best of the weather and the scenery since our arrival in Punta Arenas. At night, clear moonlight on the calm gleaming waters of the Straits. Mild temperatures and soft breezes most mornings, and in the evenings a scatter of white clouds over the harbour, but, so far, no rain. After sunset there was an occasional sharpish wind off the Straits, but hardly anything at all to suggest that we were on a coastline where terrifying gales and biting blizzards had left ships wrecked and their crews dead of cold and exposure in the fairly recent past. Summer could be a surprisingly kind season, even on the Magellan Straits.

And the penguins? Our first impression was of their tininess. The ones that bred here certainly weren't memorable for their size. There were no big jackasses or king penguins among this lot. Instead we saw sleek little creatures with short dumpy fish-and-fowl bodies and plump glistening white bellies. A cluster of them suddenly bobbed into sight along the edge of the dark-blue ocean. First they did some aquatic manoeuvres, dipping into the water and re-emerging in ones and twos, and then stood in single file along the edge of the waves as if they were naval personnel drawn up for an inspection.

Their breeding grounds were in one of the most remote places imaginable. The dirt road over the steppes gave out long before we got near the actual burrows. The minibus dropped us off beside some sand dunes and we had to walk for nearly another kilometre across a stretch of spongy mossy ground to get to the wired-off sandy fields along the shore where the penguins burrow and lay their eggs. And then, out along the Pacific itself, on a beach full of wild white breakers and impressive scatters of washed-up driftwood – big spars and logs and even a few full-length tree-trunks – the dumpy little birds surfaced suddenly out of the waves.

We must have made a comical sight. A photograph reminded me of it afterwards. A dozen or so curiosity-driven human beings sitting in a row on one of the big drifted tree-trunks, watching and waiting. And opposite us this little line of tiny bird-like fish or fish-like birds standing in a parallel row. One lot gazing at the other as if expecting something – a communication, a revelation, a miraculous little burst of mutual illumination? *¿Quién sabe?* Who knows?

Shaking the water off themselves, the line of penguins turned around in a body a few times and stood looking out towards the ocean, as if to give us a chance to inspect their plump curved posteriors, and to notice the odd little fishy tails on which they manage to balance themselves. Every so often they dived back into the sea, bobbing up and down like so many long-backed diver-ducks having a vigorous swim. Eventually they took to the deeper waters further away and disappeared behind the troughs of the huge breakers. Along the shore in the field where they laid their eggs we could see no birds at all. The rule, in any case, was not to move up too close in case of disturbing any that might be hatching.

On our way back to the city we saw several *ñandus* along with the usual flocks of grazing sheep. These tall, dusty, ungainly-looking birds were all the opposite of the smooth, curvaceous, glistening little penguins with diminutive plumage that we had just left behind along the edge of the ocean, but between them they made up an interesting set of Patagonian co-ordinates – or contrasts. Penguins can't run in any real sense of the word, and I don't suppose, from looking at them, that *ñandus* can swim even to save their lives. What these very different birds have in common is that neither of them can fly. No wonder Darwin found some parts of this continent stimulating ground for his preliminary ruminations about the evolution of species.

Las Torres del Paine, one of Chile's, and the world's, great nature reserves, is located about four hundred kilometres north of Punta Arenas in the hinterland of the small city of Puerto Natales. Our visit there was another of the many memorable moments during our journey. This park is a vast concentrated slice of some of the most scenically-spectacular landscapes in Patagonia and Chile, and maybe even in all of South America. On our way there we stopped, as most visitors do, at a spot called the *La Cueva del Milodon*. An odd pre-historic animal called the *milodon* is thought to have lived in this huge cave near Puerto Natales, as one nineteenth-century naturalist put it 'in the era before the Flood.' Fossil remains in other parts of southern Patagonia suggest a date of roughly nine thousand years before the start of the Christian era.

The *milodon* of Puerto Natales has the contradictory virtues of being a real if long-extinct animal – otherwise known as the Giant South American Sloth – while also being the subject of nearly as many mythical attributions, apocryphal sightings and speculative fantasies as the Lough Ness monster. We walked through the huge sea-cave, now situated many miles inland, and tried to imagine the gigantic, armour-plated, trunk-tailed animal who may once have lived in it. But, on the whole, we were glad not to have been around to make its acquaintance in real life.

The great National Park of Las Torres del Paine takes its name from one of the most striking features on its wild and impressive landscape. A tall cluster of jagged, tooth-like mountain blocks rears high into the sky somewhere near the centre of the park and dominates an already starkly-rugged and wildly-beautiful stretch of country. From one angle these gapped, imposing, saw-toothed peaks look like a set of gigantic broken molars. From another, you might even think they were the geologically-eroded remains of some crumbled prehistoric skyscrapers.

The park itself is immense, and we'd have needed an entire holiday to see it properly. A world of lakes, glaciers, lagoons, waterfalls, wide stretches of wind-rippled steppeland, spectacular mountains – especially those long jagged teeth of pink granite topped with black, called the Towers of Paine – it was so vast and wonderful, so full of strange plays of light and air, so fascinating in its bird, animal and plant life, that we'd have liked to stay longer, or else to come back. But we still hadn't reached the shores of Tierra del Fuego, and that, as far as I was concerned, was the real terminus of this journey.

9

A TIERRA DEL FUEGO BUS

The morning after our arrival in Punta Arenas, one of the first questions I had asked our host, Jorge Silva, was where we should go to book passages to get across the Straits to Tierra del Fuego. I felt oddly disappointed with the answer he gave me.

'There's usually no need to book a passage in advance,' he said. 'Just go down to the ferry ten minutes or so before the boat sails and you can get your tickets there. Or if you're really stuck for time you can probably buy them on the vessel itself.'

I felt an obscure sense of let-down. That seemed too casual a way, altogether, of getting to a place associated in my mind with Spanish galleons, storm-tossed schooners, and resuscitated frozen pirates. But that was how it turned out. We took the morning ferry from Punta Arenas to Porvenir on 11 February and, once we were on board, we might as well have been travelling from Roonagh to Clare Island, except that the ferry was bigger and the journey took an hour or so longer.

Porvenir is the capital of Chilean Tierra del Fuego, but still a very small town. The name Porvenir – which means 'the future' – probably expressed the hopes of its founders for some prosperous forward-looking era that they hoped the twentieth century might bring to this bleak little corner of Patagonia. But when we arrived there in February 1990, the streets and houses had a grey weather-beaten look, and the little town itself had all the signs of a struggling past and an unspectacular present. It was hard even then to imagine that it might have a prosperous future.

One of the most distinctive groups of European emigrants to arrive in this part of Patagonia, when settlement along the

Straits began to gather momentum in the early years of the twentieth century, came from Croatia and the Dalmatian regions of Yugoslavia. They worked at mining, sheep-farming, fishing or whatever else would earn them a living. Maintaining their cultural identity as a little colony, they founded the Yugoslav Club in Porvenir and their descendants still patronise it. We went in there shortly after mid-day to have an iced drink because we were already feeling hot and thirsty, although we had hardly begun our sightseeing around the little town. The shadowy interior of the Club was cool and pleasant after the very bright sunshine outside. It was turning out to be an uncomfortably hot day along the shores of Tierra del Fuego.

I wrote up my journal with my feet in the water, looking northwards towards the Chilean mainland and the rest of the world:

> A bright, clear, and amazingly hot summer's day. A few small white clouds are floating out over the Straits. The little town of Porvenir sits behind us, its grey streets brightened here and there by big clusters of ox-eye daisies. A procession from the parish church is making its way towards a small Lourdes grotto on the hill opposite the town. Long grey-green hills stretch away behind us into the distance.
>
> Further along the coast, sheep and cattle are grazing on bare-looking slopes. Wide ranges of heathery hills and boggy moorland lie behind that again. Further to the south are the towering mountains, lakes, rivers, marshlands and woods that were once the hunting-grounds of the Ona and Hausch tribes, and the haunts of their most elusive prey, the guanaco and the Patagonian fox.
>
> On a wall-map in the Yugoslav Club I've just confirmed

what I've been feeling in my bones ever since we arrived here – that this island lies in broadly the same latitude to the south of the equator as Ireland does to the north. So much for its being a short hop from here to the edge of Antarctica!

The difference is that the coasts of Tierra del Fuego, especially in the stormy south, have no big sheltering landmasses to protect them from the Antarctic winds, and, of course, there's no such thing as a warming Gulf Stream to take the edge off the freezing sub-antarctic currents. So this island gets a much rawer deal by way of unfriendly weathers than we do in Ireland. Icy gales, long snows, sub-polar blizzards, freezing fogs and the like, are familiar conditions down here, especially in the more southerly islands of the archipelago.

But not today! There's nothing cold about this part of Tierra del Fuego on this roasting-hot Sunday afternoon. In fact we might as well be steaming across some sweltering equatorial swamp, we feel so warm and sticky within a few minutes of boarding the bus in Porvenir. This serviceable little contraption travels up and down the streets of the town, detours into laneways, and stops by request at every other door to collect its passengers. If the prospective traveller isn't ready yet, it just goes ahead to the next street, picks up whoever is waiting there, and then doubles back to collect the delayed or delaying parties. A most impressive system of public transport!

But on this particular afternoon an unaccustomed heatwave was brewing up along the southern shores of the Straits. The temperature climbed and climbed until – inside the little bus at any rate – it stood somewhere around thirty degrees. The vehicle was small, tightly-packed, stuffy, and of course uncurtained, because who ever expected a sizzling hot sun and a temperature of over thirty degrees on the southern shore of the Magellan Straits? Rebecca and I peeled off all the layers we could, but still we perspired, and still the little bus picked up more passengers with bags and boxes, sacks and packages. Soon there wasn't room to breathe comfortably inside the little vehicle, never mind to get up and move around.

The last passenger to board was an old lady carrying two bulging canvas sacks, one under each arm. She had a large handbag with a cup, saucer and egg-cup sticking out of the top of it and in constant danger of falling out. Along with all that she was carrying her cat. The driver idled the engine and got down to help his elderly passenger to settle herself and her luggage as comfortably as possible into the crowded bus. He stowed her two sacks neatly away, one on top of the other, in a corner of the aisle near where she was sitting. This was something of a stevedoring feat because by now there wasn't a spare inch of space left in any part of the vehicle. When everything was in place he revved up the engine and at last we were on our way.

But not quite. Just as we were turning the corner at the top of the street, and the old lady was sitting back with the cat on her lap and the big handbag doing duty as a footstool, she realised that she had come away without her door-key. She signalled the driver to stop. She'd have to go back and find the key and lock the door because she wouldn't be coming back this way until the day after tomorrow. So the driver pulled up again, put the bus into reverse, and took her all the way back to her own doorstep. The old lady climbed out, handed me the cat, and went in to find her key and see to the security of her possessions.

By this time Rebecca and I and most of the other passengers were just about ready to melt away with the heat. But we were impressed too. So much so that, whenever I think of Tierra del

Fuego now, my most vivid memory is not of the island scenery, the black-necked swans, the great mountains, lakes and forests in the south, the blue-grey waters of the Straits, the flaming oil-rigs, the winding inlets and long heathery hills. No, I just think affectionately sometimes about the Porvenir bus.

Travellers to Tierra del Fuego in the nineteenth century didn't find things nearly so comfortable or convenient as we did. Lucas Bridges, the son of a family of English Protestant missionaries, describes the arrival of his father and mother and their oldest child at Usuhuia on the southern shores of the archipelago, after a crossing from the nearby Malvinas Islands in 1871, when they came to set up the first permanent mission settlement in Tierra del Fuego:

> The voyage from the Falklands to Tierra del Fuego was always one to be dreaded, but this trip had been worse than most. It had taken the *Allen Gardiner* forty-one days in the face of a succession of storms, or, rather, one exceptional gale with occasional short lulls when it had gathered strength for renewed attacks. On the morning of the ninth day at sea they had sighted Cape San Diego, the easternmost point of the main island of Tierra del Fuego. It was then that their real troubles had begun.
>
> Their little vessel had beaten through the Straits of Le Maire, and twice she had been driven back by stress of weather. The gales that sweep the seas around Cape Horn have an evil reputation: and few in such circumstances have passed through the Straits of Le Maire four times in one month. It is difficult to describe the mountainous waves made steeper by the world-famous 'tidal-rip' in those Straits, or the nights hove to and battened down, when the water pounds on deck or swills in the bilge, and

the creaking of timbers and spars is accompanied by the roar of the gale in the rigging, and the occasional machine-gun rattle of storm-sails when, instead of filling, they shake in the wind...

On one occasion the precious baby had been bruised, blackened and greatly frightened, when a violent jerk of the vessel had flung her from her cot into the cabin grate...

Forty-one days to get from the Falkland Islands to Tierra del Fuego must be an unenviable bad-weather and adverse-sailing record even for the days of sailing ships. But the Bridges were to get used to such hardships. They had been sent out from England to the Falklands by the Patagonian Church Missionary Society to prepare for this work in Tierra del Fuego. At the end of that stormy trip in 1871 they succeeded in setting up the island's first permanent mission colony which meant the first settlement of Europeans on the island.

They started work among the Yaganes, the most southerly of America's nomadic sea-tribes. Afterwards they made contacts and friends among the Ona and Hausch people. Their little mission-settlement at Usuhuia in the south of Tierra del Fuego was later to become the nucleus of the first civil administration established by the Argentinian government in this region of Patagonia. They were in many senses intrepid and hard-working pioneers.

The Patagonian Church Missionary Society, which sent the Bridges family to Tierra del Fuego in 1871, was typical of its time and milieu in the England of the mid-nineteenth century. The Society was founded in the 1840s, at the beginning of Queen Victoria's reign, when there was a growing swell of enthusiasm among her more religiously-minded subjects for what would later be known as the Protestant Evangelical Missionary Movement. This was, among other things, a stout-and-devout, civilising-and-proselytising, and fervently-religious expression of British imperialism.

One of the moving spirits behind the founding of the Patagonian Church Missionary Society was a former officer of the Royal Navy, Captain Allen Gardiner. He was a committed and idealistic Christian but an impetuous and unfortunate missionary. He left England in 1850 with six companions 'to convert, and turn to civilised and useful ways, the wild nomadic tribespeople of Tierra del Fuego.' But idealistic enthusiasm and passionate religious fervour are one thing. Practical planning and realistic provision for a long-term stay on an unfertile island in an exposed southern latitude would turn out to be another. The missionaries would need not only adequate food-supplies and shelter, but also guns and ammunition in order to survive on that cold uncultivated island where hunting had to be one of the main ways of securing fresh food.

When the ship which had been chartered by the Patagonian Mission Society to take them to the southern shores of Tierra del Fuego landed their provisions on the island and then sailed away to Europe again, Allen Gardiner and his companions discovered that their main supply of ammunition was not among the stores that had been unloaded. It was on its way back to England in the hold of the recently-departed ship. This meant, in effect, that they could neither hunt for meat nor defend themselves against the hungry tribespeople who began to persecute them to get at their limited store of food.

Eventually they were in such danger they had to put to sea in small boats, and try to find some remote and inaccessible part of the island to set up a more protected base. Their hope was that they might be able to hold out on strict rations until a supply-ship from the Missionary Society came out from

England again to replenish their stores. They had no idea how long that might take. With luck it could be seven or eight months, but it was more likely to be a year. In the meantime, much of their food had been stolen, their situation was exposed, and they were fugitives from the very tribespeople they had come half-way across the world to convert.

When the mission-ship arrived nearly a year later, it was confronted with a desolate scene. Allen Gardiner and his fellow-missionaries were dead. Their surviving papers and journals told a harrowing story. They had perished of cold and starvation after their little sea-cave was flooded during a storm and their small remaining store of food was lost. They died in a remote spot called Spaniard Harbour, less than a year after their arrival in Tierra del Fuego.

But Allen Gardiner was not the first Englishman to have dreamt of converting the tribespeople of Patagonia and Tierra del Fuego to Christian religion and civilised English ways. In his book *The Voyage of HMS Beagle*, Charles Darwin mentions an earlier and equally ill-fated effort:

> I have not as yet noticed the Fuegians whom we had on board. During the former voyage of *The Adventure* and *The Beagle* in 1826 to 1830, Captain Fitz Roy seized on a party of natives, as hostages for a boat which had been stolen to the great jeopardy of a party employed in the survey; and some of these natives, as well as a child whom he bought for a pearl button, he took with him to England, determining to educate them and instruct them in religion at his own expense. To settle these natives in their own country was one chief inducement to Captain Fitz Roy to undertake our present voyage...

Of the four young islanders that Fitz Roy had captured and taken with him to England in 1830, one died of small-pox in a naval hospital in Plymouth. The other three had been 'instructed in useful arts such as carpentry and gardening.' They had also been taught to speak English and to dress and comport themselves according to the best upper-class English manners of the day. They were even presented to King William and Queen Adelaide at Saint James' Palace. But that was about as far as the success of the project went.

Trying to make these three young islanders the spearhead of an evangelising and civilising English mission in Patagonia turned out to be not only unsuccessful but also, in the end, tragically counter-productive. Within months of being brought back to Tierra del Fuego in 1832, on board *The Beagle* with Fitz Roy and Darwin, the three surviving Fuegians returned to the ways and customs, dress and pursuits of their own people. That was disappointing to their captors, but to some extent it was understandable.

What seemed totally incomprehensible to their English sponsors was that the most promising and apparently civilised of the group – the young boy whom Captain Fitz Roy had bought for a pearl button and called Jemmy Button – took part in the massacre of eight missionaries of the Patagonian Church Missionary Society who landed near Wulaia in southern Tierra del Fuego in 1859 in another ill-fated attempt to set up a mission among the tribespeople. Jemmy Button and his fellow-tribesmen clubbed the missionaries to death one Sunday morning while they were singing hymns in their little chapel during a gospel service. Only one man, who was on board ship at the time, survived to tell the tale.

This violent experience was interpreted in different ways by those who reflected on it afterwards. As a last-ditch effort by the tribespeople to keep the white men out, and to preserve their freedom and age-old ways of living, according to one school of thought. As a challenging but temporary obstacle on the road to the conversion and civilisation of the wild tribes of Patagonia, according to the more fervent followers of Captains Robert Fitz Roy and Allen Gardiner.

The Patagonian Church Missionary Society wasn't an organisation to give up easily. After several attempts they eventually succeeded in setting up a stable mission on the island of Tierra del Fuego. This came about when they sent Thomas Bridges and his family to Usuhaia in 1871 in that crossing from the Falkland Islands that took forty-one days. They had prepared the way very carefully this time, and the success of the mission was due, according to Lucas Bridges, not only to his father's special human qualities – his wisdom, patience, humane leadership and absolute dedication – but also to the fact that he was following a specific missionary plan which had been carefully worked out beforehand.

The basics of this plan were found in a journal kept by Allen Gardiner during the final terrible weeks before his death by starvation in Spaniard Harbour in 1851. It acquired a kind of sacredness among missionaries of Thomas Bridges' generation because of the circumstances in which it had been prepared. Gardiner's idea was to begin missionary activity the next time, not on the island of Tierra del Fuego itself, but in a colony which was to be set up beforehand on one of the Falkland Islands.

This preparatory mission colony, which was eventually established on Keppler Island, included a school where young islanders from Tierra del Fuego were brought to be 'instructed in Christian ways and other useful skills and teachings.' Meanwhile, the prospective missionaries learned the language from the Fuegians who came to the Keppler colony, and in due course, with the help of the young people they had trained, a permanent mission settlement was set up in the south of Tierra del Fuego.

The little ship called the *Allen Gardiner* which brought the Bridges family to Usuhuia in 1871, and served afterwards as a link between the mission colonies in Usuhia and the Falkland islands, was essential to the working of the project. Even more crucial were the courage and determination of Thomas Bridges, and his sagacity and patience. He worked for the Patagonian Church Missionary Society as superintendent of the mission among the Yagan tribespeople of southern Tierra del Fuego for fifteen years. He successfully reproduced in Usuhuia the colony system that had been established beforehand in the Falklands. Then, having a family to provide for, and having come to know the southern tribespeople well, he resigned from his missionary work and became a farmer.

So the Bridges family turned out to be not only pioneers of missionary settlement in Tierra del Fuego but also one of the first white settler families from Europe to systematically farm the land on the southern and eastern shores of the island. They raised sheep and cattle, and exported meat, wool and hides to Buenos Aires, Liverpool and other markets in Europe. They also did business with the thriving new cities on the coasts of North America that were served by the Pacific Steam Navigation Company.

They secured sizeable land-grants from the Argentinian government and worked hard at clearing forests, opening up trails, and making productive use of as much as possible of the cold, swampy land of southern Tierra del Fuego. They carved out two large family *estancias*, and were eventually as successful at farming as Thomas Bridges had been in establishing the first permanent mission station on the island.

But like so much white-settler effort and civilising missionary zeal, the achievement of the Bridges family was compromised, ineluctably perhaps, by the tragic outcome of it all for the Patagonian tribes among whom they had come to work as missionaries and settled as farmers. Thomas Bridges, in his early years in Usuhuia, compiled the only known dictionary of a Patagonian tribal language. His celebrated *Yaghan Dictionary*, is a unique record of the speech of a now-extinct nomadic tribe.

The story of the Bridges family, as told by their son Lucas in a book he aptly called *Uttermost Part of the Earth* is an engaging, informative and genuinely fascinating one. It is also an important and historically-significant document. It chronicles not only the family's missionary experiences and their contacts and friendly relationships with the Patagonian tribes during the development of the first big estancias in the south of Tierra del Fuego, but it also gives us the most intimate and humane record we have of life as it was lived among the Ona, Hausch and Yaghan tribes of southern Patagonia in the decades before they finally disappeared. It is one of the few first-hand accounts we have of the interaction between two cultures that were to prove in the end – though not in the immediate experience of the Bridges family – tragically incompatible.

The Patagonian Church Missionary Society was only one of the many evangelical and proselytising organisations that flourished in Victorian England during the second half of the nineteenth century. The work of these zealous groups extended to countries in various parts of the world that the missionary societies identified as being 'outlandish, remote, and in urgent need of an evangelising and civilizing mission'. The Irish Church Mission Society appears to have decided that the west coast of Ireland, in the middle of the nineteenth-century, was such a place. When I read about Allen Gardiner's plan for setting up a mission in the Falkland islands and then in Tierra del Fuego, a bell rang somewhere in the recesses of my memory.

The purpose of most of these missionary societies was to educate young 'natives,' of whatever nationality, and turn them into 'civilized' Christians of a distinctively English Protestant cut. It didn't seem to matter that this might not be a sensible, much less a sensitive way to help them to live with freedom and dignity on their own very un-English landscapes. The particular memory that Allen Gardiner's plan brought to my mind was a story I had heard as a child about events that took place on the west coast of Mayo a few generations before I was born.

About the time that the Patagonian Church Missionary Society was busy with its evangelising project in Keppler Island and Tierra del Fuego, the Irish Church Mission Society was engaged in setting up a number of similar colonies in west Mayo. One of these was located a few miles west of Louisburgh in a village where a branch of the MacHale family, cousins of my great-grandfather, lived. Bitter memories of that colony and the misplaced zeal of its workers were part of the experience of many families in the area during those poverty-ridden years. Some of those experiences were so divisive and humiliating that – like the terrible events of the Black Famine in the 1840s – they were seldom spoken openly about until a great many years afterwards. My mother, who was born in 1893, knew families who had had personal experience of the Irish Church Mission colony, and she knew some old people who had been pupils in the school there when they were children. She told me the following story.

A young woman, a cousin of the MacHale family, was married to a man called Tony. As far as I remember she never mentioned Tony's surname. They had a big family, and a small holding of poor land which was the property of Lord Sligo. When the famine struck in the middle of the 1840s and came back again twice during the decades that followed, they were in desperate straits and often close to starvation. Their relatives and neighbours helped them as best they could, but Tony was a proud and obstinate man, who swore that he would not be beholden to his wife's relations for bread to put in his children's mouths. So he went to the local Irish Church Mission colony and asked for help for his hungry family. In return for converting to the Protestant religion, which involved attending services in Saint Catherine's Church in Louisburgh on Sundays and sending his children to the colony school, he was given the immediate help he needed.

As a result, the family became known as 'Jumpers'. This was a disrespectful term used in the west of Ireland during those years to describe poor people who 'jumped' over to the Protestant religion to get food and help in time of need. The word carried pejorative connotations from the Irish language too. An expression from the same era said *d'iompaigh siad*, meaning they changed their religion for material help. The fact that most of those poor people jumped back again to their original church as soon as the crisis was over only added to the ostracisation and humiliation they had to face from their neighbours and fellow-parishioners. Many of the latter believed that they had felt the pinch just as much but had somehow managed to hold out against the tempting bait, and they tended to look down on the others.

So Tony 'jumped,' but his wife didn't, and there was conflict and bitterness in their family from then onwards. The proselytising of her children in the nearby colony school was the hardest thing for the mother to bear. It preyed on her mind and affected her health to such an extent that she became ill, and died soon afterwards, as my mother put it, of a broken heart. She was only in her mid-forties. On her deathbed she asked for the Catholic priest in Louisburgh to come out and give her the last sacraments, but her husband refused to send for him and swore he'd never allow a Catholic clergyman inside the door of his house again. So the dying woman sent one of her children secretly to her brother's house and asked him to go into Louisburgh and bring out the priest. A few hours later the parish priest arrived on horseback from the town, but when he tried to get into the house to administer the last sacraments to the dying woman, Tony stood defiantly in the doorway and barred his entry with a pitchfork. His wife died a few hours later without the consolation of her church's last rites.

The story had a sequel which was also painful. Immediately after their mothers' death, the youngest children, two little girls, were taken away to the Crow's Nest which was the local name for the Irish Church Mission Orphanage on the other side of the bay in Achill. As a child I was innocent enough to think that this part of the story was exciting because it involved a daring rescue by sea at night.

Two men of the MacHale family decided to get the children out of the Crow's Nest. They rowed down across Clew Bay to Achill and landed after dark in a cove a few miles from the orphanage. They waited patiently until one of them found a way of getting into the building. Under cover of darkness he smuggled the two little girls out and took them to where his boat was waiting. They rowed away again into the night and brought the children back with them. But there was a sad sequel to that part of the story too. Because of the continuing conflict between the families, the children were put into the Catholic orphanage in Westport for protection.

We have no records and, of course, no transmitted oral memories, to tell us if the Yaghan or Ona or Hausch people of Tierra del Fuego suffered the intimate sting of that kind of family division and humiliation as a result of their dealings with the missionaries who came to their island from Europe in the late nineteenth century. What we do know of their interaction with the missionaries is tragic in another way. The mission colonies, in spite of the best efforts of those who ran them, became unwitting instruments in the annihilation of the Patagonian tribes, because they were the places where common European diseases and epidemics, against which the tribespeople had no immunity, spread like wildfire and wiped out thousands of the islanders.

And what the epidemics didn't do, the more ruthless of the white settlers finished off in their own way. They made outlaws of the Patagonian tribespeople on their ancestral lands. In some cases they even treated them as prey to be hunted down and exterminated. What seems difficult to believe is that this happened less than a hundred years ago, and that the protagonists were, in their own view, standard-bearers of European progress and civilisation. It was hardly surprising that one of the darker threads that ran through Rebecca's conversations with me during this journey, and on other occasions as well, was the cruel treatment that we Europeans meted out to the indigenous peoples in so many countries of this hemisphere over the centuries.

Men and women of the wind! There's an almost inexpressible sadness about the story of the native peoples of Patagonia and their relatively recent disappearance from the face of the earth, just as there's an awesome remoteness still about the cold territories where, for so long, they managed to survive. Writing about the conquering armies of the Roman Empire many centuries ago, one of their own historians said, 'They created a desert and called it peace.' There are many people in South America today whose view of us Europeans is that we created a collective grave and called it civilisation.

10

ALONG THE RIM OF THE PACIFIC

There's something almost like unfinished business about fulfilling your dream, climbing your mountain, reaching your island – and then coming back. What follows is often the most difficult part, taking the road home and getting on with some ordinary life again. But, for me, after my journey to Tierra del Fuego, there wasn't, for the moment, any familiar life to get back to. As I stood on the deck of the *Tierra del Fuego* at the end of February 1990, and watched the dark waters of Patagonia closing in a frothy wake behind our north-bound ship, I knew that this was a decisive moment in my own life. I had fulfilled my childhood dream, and reached and left behind me the mythical shores of Tierra del Fuego. My personal journey, however, was at this moment bound up with a transition from Europe to South America and from Ireland to Chile that was still very much in progress. It was not firmly accomplished yet. I was still trying, as Zbigniew Herbert put it, 'to be faithful to uncertain clarity.'

But during the time we had spent in Patagonia, I realised that a subtle change had been happening for me. A gradual shift of focus had begun to take place, as if I had become convinced at some deep level that what I must look to now was not what I was leaving behind me, whether that was in Europe or Ireland or Dublin, but what I might dedicate my energies to in the future. It would still be a struggle. I'd still have to push my tiny craft out into some wide unknown waters again. But something – which was beyond my power to articulate at that moment – convinced me that the venture would be both possible and worthwhile.

Back in Valparaiso, I watched the children returning to school after the long summer holidays with shiny shoes and pressed uniforms, entering hopefully on another school year. I felt ready for a new beginning too. Some sense of confidence and clarity had quietly come to birth in me during the later stages of the voyage to Patagonia. Some lesson from that wild landscape and the tragedy of its vanished tribespeople seemed to have an intimate bearing on my own life. Within a few days of my return I posted the letter to my family and friends telling them that I was leaving Ireland and community life in Dublin to settle on my own in Valparaiso.

I knew by then that whatever the outcome of things in Carysfort, I was fortunate to have lived and worked there. The sale of the college – until I saw a university business-school taking shape on the campus some years later – saddened and puzzled me. But the journey to Patagonia had brought me face to face with so many things that were transient, worlds and people whose loss was far more poignant for humanity than the passing of a college that, when all was said and done, had fulfilled its purpose, served its society well, and belonged essentially to an age that was over.

In March 1999 I celebrated ten years of living what – for want of a better term – I tend to think of as a semi-hermit's life on a poor hill in Valparaíso. As I sat on my little terrace that morning and looked out over the blue-grey reaches of the Pacific, I was conscious of a deep sense of gratitude, not only for the ten years in Chile but for the five decades that went before them as well.

Afterwards I spent the day as I usually do: a few hours at the desk, some time with the students over lunch, a walk to the sea, a visit to an elderly neighbour, a call to the post-office where I found a bank-statement from Ireland telling me that my Help for Children Account needs replenishing. Its regular sources –

pension savings, royalties and occasional gifts from friends – barely meet the recurring commitments.

So a semi-hermit's life is not, on the face of it, a very exciting business. The television team who visited Valparaíso recently to make a documentary film about my life in Chile found this a challenge. How can a camera penetrate to the secret spaces where seminal things are happening in a person's life? How can it reach the nebulous thoughts that may take shape afterwards in such decisive and unexpected ways?

If you focus on a small girl sitting on a rock watching the sun setting over the Atlantic, how can you tell that she's starting on a journey to the rim of the Pacific? How can you guess she's thinking about a faraway island called Tierra del Fuego? And that it doesn't matter if it takes her a long time to get there, because she intends to follow the path of the sun across those shimmering waters anyway? How can she tell you any of this when she hardly knows it yet, herself?

Playa Ancha, Valparaíso
July 1999